The Caucasian Chalk Circle

In the Prologue, delegates from two collective farms in the Caucasus meet to decide which shall take over a valley devastated by Hitler's armies. After their discussion a local singer and his musicians entertain them with the story of the Chalk Circle, which is the play proper. The first part describes a revolt in feudal Georgia and the flight to the mountains of Grusha, a servant girl, with the Governor's small son who has been abandoned in the panic by his mother; in the second part a drunken village clerk, Azdak, is made a judge by the rebellious soldiers and tries the case.

The play was written in America in 1944-45 and was first performed there in English. The first performance in Germany was in 1954 in a production by Brecht, with his wife Helene Weigel as the Governor's Wife.

The photograph on the front of the cover shows a scene from the 1954 production in the Theater am Schiffbauerdamm, Berlin, and is reproduced by courtesy of the Berliner Ensemble. The photograph on the back is reproduced by courtesy of Gerda Goedhart.

The Caucasian Chalk Circle

BY

BERTOLT BRECHT

translated by
James and Tania Stern,
with W. H. Auden

LONDON
METHUEN & CO LTD
11 NEW FETTER LANE · EC4

1.3
Paperback edition first published in June 1963
reprinted 1965 *and* 1966
This translation copyright © (*Act* 5) 1946 *and* 1960
by James and Tania Stern and W. H. Auden;
original work published under the title of
DER KAUKASISCHE KREIDEKREIS
copyright 1954 *by Suhrkamp Verlag, Berlin*
Printed in Great Britain by
Robert Cunningham and Sons Ltd
Alva, Clackmannanshire
Cat. No. 02/6305/24

The Caucasian Chalk Circle

COLLABORATOR: R. Berlau

TRANSLATORS: James and Tania Stern, with W. H. Auden

MUSIC: Paul Dessau

Written in 1944-45. First produced in English (Eric Bentley's
translation) at Nourse Little Theatre, Northfield, Minnesota,
U.S.A., on 4 May 1948

CHARACTERS

*An old peasant and peasant woman on the right: a young peasant:
a very young workman: an old peasant and peasant woman on the
left: the agriculturist: the girl tractor driver: the wounded soldier:
other peasants from the kolchos: the expert from the capital: the
singer, Arkadi Tsheidse: his musicians: Georgi Abashvili, the
Governor: his wife, Natella: their son, Michael: Shalva, the
adjutant: Arsen Kazbeki, the fat prince: the rider from the
capital: Niko Mikadze and Mikha Loladze, doctors: Simon
Chachava, a soldier: Grusha Vachnadze, a kitchenmaid: three
architects: four chambermaids — Assia, Masha, Sulika and Fat
Nina: a nurse: a cook: a stableman: servants in the governor's
palace: the governor's and the fat prince's Ironshirts and soldiers:
beggars and petitioners: the old peasant with the milk: two elegant
ladies: the innkeeper: the servant: a corporal: 'Blockhead', a
soldier: a peasant woman and her husband: three merchants:
Lavrenti Vachnadze, Grusha's brother: his wife, Aniko: their
stableman: the peasant woman, for a time Grusha's mother-in-
law: Yussup, her son: Brother Anastasius, a monk: wedding guests:
children: Azdak, the village clerk: Shauva, a policeman: a
refugee, the Grand Duke: the doctor: the invalid: the limping man:
the blackmailer: Ludovica, the innkeeper's daughter-in-law: a
poor old peasant woman: her brother-in-law Irakli, a bandit: three
farmers: Illo Shaboladze and Sandro Oboladze, lawyers: the
very old married couple.*

I

THE STRUGGLE FOR THE VALLEY

Among the ruins of a destroyed Caucasian village the members of two kolchos villages are sitting in a circle, smoking and drinking wine. They consist mainly of women and old men, but there are also a few soldiers among them. With them is an expert of the Federal Reconstruction Commission from the capital.

A PEASANT WOMAN *left, pointing*: In those hills over there we stopped three Nazi tanks. But the apple orchard had already been destroyed.

AN OLD PEASANT *right*: Our beautiful dairy farm. All in ruins.

A GIRL TRACTOR DRIVER *left*: I set fire to it, Comrade.

Pause.

THE EXPERT: Now listen to the report: the delegates of the goat-breeding kolchos 'Galinsk' have arrived in Nukha. When the Hitler armies were approaching, the kolchos had been ordered by the authorities to move its goat-herds further to the east. The kolchos now considers resettling in this valley. Its delegates have investigated the village and the grounds and found a high degree of destruction. *The delegates on the right nod.* The neighbouring fruit-growing kolchos 'Rosa Luxemburg' – *to the left* – moves that the former grazing land of the 'Galinsk' kolchos, a valley with scanty growth of grass, should be used for the replanting of orchards and vineyards. As an expert of the Reconstruction Commission, I request the two kolchos villages to decide between themselves whether the 'Galinsk' kolchos shall return here or not.

AN OLD MAN *right*: First of all, I want to protest against the restriction of time for discussion. We of the 'Galinsk' kolchos have spent three days and three nights getting here. And now we are allowed a discussion of only half a day.

A WOUNDED SOLDIER *left*: Comrade, we no longer have as many villages and no longer as many working hands and no longer as much time.

THE GIRL TRACTOR DRIVER *left*: All pleasures have to be rationed. Tobacco is rationed, and wine and discussion, too.

THE OLD MAN *right, sighing*: Death to the Fascists! But I will come to the point and explain to you why we want to have our valley back. There are a great many reasons, but I want to begin with one of the simplest. Makinae Abakidze, unpack the goat cheese.

A peasant woman, right, takes from a basket an enormous cheese wrapped in a cloth. Applause and laughter.

Help yourselves, comrades. Start in.

AN OLD PEASANT *left, suspiciously*: Is this meant to influence us, perhaps?

THE OLD MAN *right, amidst laughter*: How could it be meant as an influence, Surab, you valley-thief? Everyone knows that you will take the cheese and the valley, too. *Laughter*. All I expect from you is an honest answer: Do you like the cheese?

THE OLD MAN *left*: The answer is yes.

THE OLD MAN *right*: Oh. *Bitterly*. I might have guessed you know nothing about cheese.

THE OLD MAN *left*: Why not? When I tell you I like it!

THE OLD MAN *right*: Because you can't like it. Because it's not what it was in the old days. And why isn't it? Because our goats don't like the new grass as they used to like the old. Cheese is not cheese because grass is not grass, that's it. Mind you put that in your report.

THE OLD MAN *left*: But your cheese is excellent.

THE OLD MAN *right*: It's not excellent. Barely decent. The new grazing land is no good, whatever the young people may say. I tell you, it's impossible to live there. It doesn't even smell of morning there in the morning.

Several people laugh.

THE EXPERT: Don't mind their laughter. They understand you

4

all the same. Comrades, why does one love one's country? Because the bread tastes better there, the sky is higher, the air smells better, voices sound stronger, the ground is easier to walk on. Isn't that so?

THE OLD MAN *right*: The valley has belonged to us for centuries.

THE SOLDIER *left*: What does that mean – for centuries? Nothing belongs to anyone for centuries. When you were young you didn't even belong to yourself, but to Prince Kazbeki.

THE OLD MAN *right*: According to the law the valley belongs to us.

THE GIRL TRACTOR DRIVER: The laws will have to be re-examined in any case, to see whether they are still valid.

THE OLD MAN *right*: That's obvious. You mean to say it makes no difference what kind of tree stands beside the house where one was born? Or what kind of neighbour one has? Doesn't that make any difference? We want to go back just to have you as neighbours in our kolchos, you valley-thieves. Now you can laugh again.

THE OLD MAN *left*, *laughing*: Then why don't you listen to what your 'neighbour', Kato Wachtang, our agriculturist, has to say about the valley?

A PEASANT WOMAN *right*: We haven't said anywhere near all we have to say about our valley. Not all the houses are destroyed. At least the foundation wall of the dairy farm is still standing.

THE EXPERT: You can claim State support – both here and there. You know that.

A PEASANT WOMAN *right*: Comrade Expert, we're not trading now. I can't take your cap and hand you another, and say: 'This one's better.' The other one might be better, but you prefer yours.

THE GIRL TRACTOR DRIVER: A piece of land is not like a cap. Not in our country, comrade.

THE EXPERT: Don't get angry. It's true that we have to consider a piece of land as a tool with which one produces something useful. But it's also true that we must recognize the love for a particular piece of land. Before we continue the discussion I suggest that you explain to the comrades of the 'Galinsk' kolchos just what you intend to do with the disputed valley.

THE OLD MAN *right*: Agreed.

THE OLD MAN *left*: Yes, let Kato speak.

THE EXPERT: Comrade Agriculturist!

THE AGRICULTURIST *rising. She is in military uniform*: Last winter, Comrades, while we were fighting here in these hills as partisans, we discussed how after the expulsion of the Germans we could increase our orchards to ten times their former size. I have prepared the plan for an irrigation project. With the help of a coffer-dam on our mountain lake, three hundred hectares of unfertile land can be irrigated. Our kolchos could then grow not only more fruit, but wine as well. The project, however, would pay only if the disputed valley of the 'Galinsk' kolchos could also be included. Here are the calculations. *She hands the expert a briefcase.*

THE OLD MAN *right*: Write into the report that our kolchos plans to start a new stud farm.

THE GIRL TRACTOR DRIVER: Comrades, the project was conceived during the days and nights when we had to take cover in the mountains and often were without ammunition for our few rifles. Even to get a pencil was difficult.

Applause from both sides.

THE OLD MAN *right*: Our thanks to the comrades of the 'Rosa Luxemburg' kolchos and to all those who defended our country.

They shake hands and embrace.

THE PEASANT WOMAN *left*: Our thoughts were that our soldiers – both your men and our men – should return to a still more fertile homeland.

THE GIRL TRACTOR DRIVER: As the poet Mayakovski said: 'The home of the Soviet people shall also be the home of Reason!'

The delegates on the right (except the old man) have risen and, with the expert, study the agriculturist's plans. Exclamations such as: 'Why is there a fall of 66 feet?' – 'This rock here is to be dynamited!' – 'Actually, all they need is cement and dynamite!' – 'They force the water to come down here, that's clever!'

A VERY YOUNG WORKMAN *right, to the old man, right*: They are
    going to irrigate all the fields between the hills – look at that,
    Alleko.

THE OLD MAN *right*: I am not going to look at it. I knew the
    project would be good. I won't have a revolver pointed at my
    chest.

THE SOLDIER: But they are only pointing a pencil at your chest.

Laughter.

THE OLD MAN *right. He gets up gloomily and walks over to look at
    the drawings*: These valley-thieves know only too well that
    we can't resist machines and projects in this country.

THE PEASANT WOMAN *right*: Alleko Bereshvili, you yourself
    are the worst one at new projects. That is well known.

THE EXPERT: What about my report? May I write that in your
    kolchos you will support the transfer of your old valley for
    the project?

THE PEASANT WOMAN *right*: I will support it. What about you,
    Alleko?

THE OLD MAN *right, bent over the drawings*: I move that you
    give us copies of the drawings to take along.

THE PEASANT WOMAN *right*: Then we can sit down to eat. Once
    he has the drawings and is ready to discuss them, the affair is
    settled. I know him. And it will be the same with the rest of us.

The delegates embrace again amidst laughter.

THE OLD MAN *left*: Long live the 'Galinsk' kolchos and good
    luck to your new stud farm!

THE PEASANT WOMAN *left*: Comrades, in honour of the visit of
    the delegates from the 'Galinsk' kolchos and of the expert we
    have arranged a play featuring the singer Arkadi Tsheidse,
    which has some bearing on our problem.

Applause.
The girl tractor driver has gone off to fetch the singer.

THE PEASANT WOMAN *right*: Comrades, your play will have to
    be good. We're going to pay for it with a valley.

THE PEASANT WOMAN *left*: Arkadi Tsheidse knows 21,000 verses by heart.

THE OLD MAN *left*: We rehearsed the play under his direction. It is very difficult to get him, by the way. You and the Planning Commission should see to it that he comes north more often, comrade.

THE EXPERT: We are more concerned with economy.

THE OLD MAN *left, smiling*: You arrange the new distribution of grapevines and tractors. Why not of songs, too?

Enter the singer Arkadi Tsheidse, led by the girl tractor driver. He is a sturdy man of simple manners, accompanied by musicians with their instruments. The artistes are greeted with applause.

THE GIRL TRACTOR DRIVER: This is the comrade expert, Arkadi.

The singer greets those round him.

THE PEASANT WOMAN *right*: I am very honoured to make your acquaintance. I've heard about your songs ever since I was at school.

THE SINGER: This time it's a play with songs, and almost the whole kolchos takes part. We have brought along the old masks.

THE OLD MAN *right*: Is it going to be one of the old legends?

THE SINGER: A very old one. It is called 'The Chalk Circle' and is derived from the Chinese. But we will recite it in a changed version. Yura, show the masks. Comrades, we consider it an honour to entertain you after such a difficult debate. We hope you will find that the voice of the old poet also sounds well in the shadow of the Soviet tractors. It may be mistaken to mix different wines, but old and new wisdom mix very well. Now I hope we will all be given something to eat before the recital begins. That usually helps.

VOICES: Of course. – Everyone into the club house.

All go cheerfully to the meal. While they begin to move off, the expert turns to the singer.

THE EXPERT: How long will the story take, Arkadi? I have to get back to Tiflis tonight.

8

THE SINGER *casually*: It is actually two stories. A few hours.
THE EXPERT *very confidentially*: Couldn't you make it shorter?
THE SINGER: No.

2

THE NOBLE CHILD

THE SINGER, *who is seen sitting on the floor in front of his musicians,
a black sheepskin cloak round his shoulders, leafing through a
small, well-thumbed notebook*:

Once upon a time
A time of bloodshed
When this city was called
The city of the damned
It had a Governor.
His name was Georgi Abashvili
Once upon a time.

He was very rich
He had a beautiful wife
He had a healthy child
Once upon a time.

No other governor in Grusinia
Had as many horses in his stable
As many beggars on his doorstep
As many soldiers in his service
As many petitioners in his courtyard
Once upon a time.

Georgi Abashvili, how shall I describe him?
He enjoyed his life:
On Easter Sunday morning
The Governor and his family went to church
Once upon a time.

Beggars and petitioners stream from a palace gateway, holding up thin children, crutches, and petitions. They are followed by two Ironshirts and then by the Governor's family, elaborately dressed.

THE BEGGARS AND PETITIONERS: Mercy, Your Grace, the taxes are beyond our means. . . I lost my leg in the Persian War, where can I get . . . My brother is innocent, Your Grace, a misunderstanding . . . My child is starving in my arms . . . We plead for our son's discharge from the army, our one remaining son . . . Please, Your Grace, the water inspector is corrupt.

A servant collects the petitions, another distributes coins from a purse. Soldiers push back the crowd, lashing at it with thick leather whips.

SOLDIER: Get back! Make way at the church door!

Behind the Governor, his wife and his Adjutant, the Governor's child is driven through the gateway in an ornate little carriage. The crowd surges forward to see it.

THE CROWD: The child! . . . I can't see it, stop pushing! . . . God bless the child, Your Grace!
THE SINGER *while the crowd is driven back with whips*:
      For the first time on this Easter Sunday, the people see the heir.
      Two doctors never leave the child, the noble child
      Apple of the Governor's eye.
      Even the mighty Prince Kazbeki
      Bows before it at the church door.

A fat prince steps forward and bows before the family.

THE FAT PRINCE: Happy Easter, Natella Abashvili!

A command is heard. A rider arrives at the gallop and holds out to the Governor a roll of documents. At a nod from the Governor the Adjutant, a handsome young man, approaches the rider and stops him. There follows a brief pause during which the fat prince eyes the rider suspiciously.

THE FAT PRINCE: What a magnificent day! While it was raining in the night I thought to myself: gloomy holidays. But this morning: a gay sky. I love a bright sky, a simple heart, Natella Abashvili. And little Michael, a governor from head to foot, tititi! *He tickles the child.* Happy Easter, little Michael, tititi!

THE GOVERNOR'S WIFE: What do you think of this, Arsen? Georgi has finally decided to start building the new wing on the east side. All these miserable slum houses are to be torn down to make room for a garden.

THE FAT PRINCE: That's good news after so much bad. What's the latest about the war, Brother Georgi? *The Governor shows his lack of interest.* A strategic retreat, I hear? Well, minor reverses invariably occur. Sometimes things go well, sometimes not so well. Such are the fortunes of war. Doesn't mean much, eh?

THE GOVERNOR'S WIFE: He's coughing! Georgi, did you hear? *Sharply to the two doctors, dignified men, who stand close to the little carriage*: He's coughing!

FIRST DOCTOR *to the second*: May I remind you, Niko Mikadze, that I was against the lukewarm bath? A minor oversight in warming the bath water, Your Grace.

SECOND DOCTOR *equally polite*: I can't possibly agree with you, Mikha Loladze. The temperature of the bath water was the one prescribed by our great and beloved Mishiko Oboladze. More likely a slight draught in the night, Your Grace.

THE GOVERNOR'S WIFE: But do take better care of him. He looks feverish, Georgi.

FIRST DOCTOR *bending over the child*: No cause for alarm, Your Grace. The bath water will be warmer. It won't happen again.

SECOND DOCTOR *with a poisonous glance at the first*: I won't forget it, dear Mikha Loladze. No cause for alarm, Your Grace.

THE FAT PRINCE: Well, well, well! I always say: one pain in my liver and the doctor gets fifty strokes on the soles of his feet. And that's only because we live in such a decadent age. In the old days it would have been: Off with his head!

THE GOVERNOR'S WIFE: Let's go into the church. Very likely it's the draught here.

The procession, consisting of the family and servants, turns into the church doorway. The fat prince follows. The Adjutant leaves the procession and points at the rider.

THE GOVERNOR: Not before divine service, Shalva.

ADJUTANT *to the rider*: The Governor doesn't want to be bothered with reports before the service – especially if they are, as I suspect, of a depressing nature. Go and get yourself something to eat in the kitchen, my friend.

The Adjutant joins the procession while the rider enters the palace gateway, cursing. A soldier appears from the palace and remains standing in the gateway.

THE SINGER:

The city lies still.
On the church square the pigeons preen themselves.
A soldier of the palace guard
Is jesting with the kitchen maid
As she comes up from the river with a bundle.

A girl tries to pass through the gateway, a bundle of large green leaves under her arm.

THE SOLDIER: What! The young lady is not in church? Shirking service?

GRUSHA: I was already dressed to go. But they wanted one more goose for the Easter banquet. And they asked me to fetch it. I know something about geese.

THE SOLDIER: A goose? *Feigning suspicion.* I'd like to see that goose.

Grusha doesn't understand.

One has to be on one's guard with women. They say: 'I only went to fetch a goose', and then it turns out to be something quite different.

GRUSHA *walks resolutely towards him and shows him the goose*: There it is. And if it isn't a fifteen-pound goose, and they haven't stuffed it with corn, I'll eat the feathers.

THE SOLDIER: A queen of a goose. It will be eaten by the Governor himself. So the young lady has been down to the river again?

GRUSHA: Yes, at the poultry farm.

THE SOLDIER: I see! At the poultry farm, down by the river. Not higher up, near those – those willows?

GRUSHA: I only go to the willows to wash linen.

THE SOLDIER *insinuatingly*: Exactly.

GRUSHA: Exactly what?

THE SOLDIER *winking*: Exactly that.

GRUSHA: Why shouldn't I wash my linen near the willows?

THE SOLDIER *with exaggerated laughter*: 'Why shouldn't I wash my linen near the willows!' That's a good one, that is!

GRUSHA: I don't understand the soldier. What's so good about it?

THE SOLDIER *slyly*: If someone knew what someone's told, she'd grow hot, she'd grow cold.

GRUSHA: I don't know what I could know about those willows.

THE SOLDIER: Not even if there were a bush opposite? From which everything could be seen? Everything that happens there when a certain person is washing linen?

GRUSHA: What happens there? Won't the soldier say what he means and have done with it?

THE SOLDIER: Something happens. And perhaps something can be seen.

GRUSHA: Could the soldier mean that – once in a while on a hot day – I put my toes in the water? For otherwise there's nothing.

THE SOLDIER: And more – the toes and more.

GRUSHA: More what? At most the foot.

THE SOLDIER: The foot and a little more. *He laughs heartily.*

GRUSHA *angrily*: Simon Chachava, you ought to be ashamed of yourself! To sit in a bush on a hot day and wait till someone comes along and puts her leg in the river! And most likely with another soldier! *She runs off.*

THE SOLDIER *shouting after her*: Not with another soldier!

As the singer resumes his story the soldier runs after Grusha.

THE SINGER:

> The city lies still, but why are there armed men?
> The Governor's palace lies at peace
> But why is it a fortress?

From the doorway at the left the fat prince enters quickly. He stands still and looks around. Before the gateway at the right two Iron-shirts are waiting. Noticing them, the prince walks slowly past them, signs to them, then exits quickly. One Ironshirt exits through the gateway, the other remains on guard. Muffled voices come from different sides in the rear: 'To your posts!' The palace is sur-rounded. Distant church bells. Enter through the doorway the pro-cession and the Governor's family returning from church.

THE SINGER:

> Then the Governor returned to his palace
> Then the fortress was a trap
> Then the goose was cooked and spiced
> Then the goose was no longer eaten
> Then noon was no longer the hour to eat
> Then noon was the hour to die.

THE GOVERNOR'S WIFE *in passing*: It's quite impossible to live in this slum. But Georgi, of course, builds only for his little Michael. Never for me. Michael is everything, everything for Michael!

THE GOVERNOR: Did you hear Brother Kazbeki bid me a 'Happy Easter'? That's all very well, but so far as I know it didn't rain in Nukha last night. It rained where Brother Kazbeki was. Where was Brother Kazbeki?

THE ADJUTANT: That will have to be investigated.

THE GOVERNOR: Yes, at once. Tomorrow.

The procession turns into the gateway. The rider, who has mean-while returned from the palace, walks towards the Governor.

THE ADJUTANT: Don't you want to listen to the rider from the capital, Your Excellency? He arrived this morning with con-fidential papers.

THE GOVERNOR *in passing*: Not before the banquet, Shalva!

THE ADJUTANT *to the rider, while the procession disappears into*

14

the palace and only two Ironshirts remain at the gate as palace guards: The Governor doesn't wish to be disturbed by military reports before the banquet. The afternoon His Excellency will devote to conferences with prominent architects who have also been invited to the banquet. Here they are already. *Enter three men. As the rider goes off, the Adjutant greets the architects.* Gentlemen, His Excellency is awaiting you at the banquet. His entire time will be devoted to you. To the great new plans! Come, let us go!

ONE OF THE ARCHITECTS: We are amazed that his Excellency thinks of building. There are disquieting rumours that the war in Persia has taken a turn for the worse.

THE ADJUTANT: All the more reason for building! That's nothing. Persia is far away. The garrison here would let itself be chopped to pieces for its Governor.

Uproar from the palace. Shrill screams of a woman. Orders are shouted. Dumbfounded, the Adjutant moves towards the gateway. An Ironshirt steps out and holds him up at the point of a lance.

What's going on here? Put down that lance, you dog! *To the palace guard, furiously.* Lay down your arms. Can't you see an attempt is being made on the Governor's life?

The palace guard Ironshirts refuse to obey. Staring coldly, indifferently, at the Adjutant, they watch the proceedings without interest. The Adjutant fights his way into the palace.

ONE OF THE ARCHITECTS: The Princes! Don't you realise that the Princes met last night in the capital? And that they are against the Grand Duke and his governors? Gentlemen, we'd better make ourselves scarce.

They rush off.

THE SINGER:

Oh, blindness of the great! They walk like gods
Great over bent backs, sure
Of hired fists, trusting
In their power which has already lasted so long.
But long is not forever.
Oh, Wheel of Fortune! Hope of the people!

From the gateway, enter the Governor with a grey face, manacled, between two soldiers armed to the teeth.

> Walk, Your Highness, walk even now with head up.
> From your Palace the eyes of many foes follow you!
> You no longer need an architect, a carpenter will do.
> You will not move into a new palace, but into a little hole
>   in the ground.
> Just look about you once more, you blind man!

The arrested Governor looks about him.

> Does all you once possessed still please you? Between the
>   Easter Mass and the banquet
> You are walking to that place from which no one returns.

The Governor is led away. The palace guard follows. A horn sounds. Noise behind the gateway.

> When the houses of the great collapse
> Many little people are slain.
> Those who had no share in the fortunes of the mighty
> Often have a share in their misfortunes. The plunging
>   wain
> Drags the sweating beasts with it into the abyss.

Servants come rushing through the gateway in panic.

THE SERVANTS *in confusion*: The hampers! – Take them all into the third courtyard! Food for five days! – Her Ladyship has fainted! Someone must carry her down. She must get away. – And what about us? We'll be slaughtered like chickens, it's the old story. – Jesus and Mary, what's going to happen? There's already bloodshed in the town, they say. – Nonsense, the Governor has just been asked politely to appear at a Princes' meeting. Everything'll be all right. I have this on the best authority.

The two doctors rush into the courtyard.

FIRST DOCTOR *trying to restrain the other*: Niko Mikadze, it is your duty as a doctor to attend Natella Abashvili.
SECOND DOCTOR: My duty? It's yours!

FIRST DOCTOR: Niko Mikadze, who is in charge of the child today? You or me?

SECOND DOCTOR: Do you really think, Mikha Loladze, I'm going to stay another minute in this cursèd house for that little brat?

They start fighting. All one hears is: 'You neglect your duty!' and 'Duty be damned!' Then the second doctor knocks down the first.

SECOND DOCTOR: Oh, go to hell! *Exit.*

THE SERVANTS: There's time enough before night. The soldiers won't be drunk till then. – Does anyone know if they've started a mutiny yet? – The Palace Guard has ridden away. – Doesn't anyone know what's happened?

GRUSHA: Meliva the fisherman says a comet with a red tail has been seen in the sky over the capital. That means bad luck.

THE SERVANTS: Yesterday they were saying in the capital that the Persian War is lost. – The Princes have started a great revolt. There's a rumour that the Grand Duke has already fled. All his Governors are to be hanged. – The likes of us will be left alone. I have a brother with the Ironshirts.

Enter the soldier Simon Chachava, searching the crowd for Grusha.

THE ADJUTANT *appearing in the doorway*: Everyone into the third courtyard! All hands help with the packing!

He drives the servants out. Simon finally finds Grusha.

SIMON: There you are at last, Grusha! What are you going to do?

GRUSHA: Nothing. If the worst comes to the worst, I've a brother with a farm in the mountains. But what about you?

SIMON: Don't worry about me. *Polite again.* Grusha Vachnadze, your desire to know my plans fills me with satisfaction. I've been ordered to accompany Madam Natella Abashvili as her guard.

GRUSHA: But hasn't the Palace Guard mutinied?

SIMON *serious*: That's a fact.

GRUSHA: But isn't it dangerous to accompany the woman?

SIMON: In Tiflis they say: Isn't the stabbing dangerous for the knife?

GRUSHA: You're not a knife. You're a man, Simon Chachava. What has this woman to do with you?

SIMON: The woman has nothing to do with me. But I have my orders, and so I go.

GRUSHA: The soldier is a pig-headed man; he gets himself into danger for nothing – nothing at all. *As she is called from the palace:* Now I must go into the third courtyard. I'm in a hurry.

SIMON: As there's a hurry we oughtn't to quarrel. For a good quarrel one needs time. May I ask if the young lady still has parents?

GRUSHA: No, only a brother.

SIMON: As time is short – the second question would be: Is the young lady as healthy as a fish in water?

GRUSHA: Perhaps once in a while a pain in the right shoulder; but otherwise strong enough for any work. So far no one has complained.

SIMON: Everyone knows that. Even if it's Easter Sunday and there's the question who shall fetch the goose, then it's she. The third question is this: Is the young lady impatient? Does she want cherries in winter?

GRUSHA: Impatient, no. But if a man goes to war without any reason, and no message comes, that's bad.

SIMON: A message will come. *Grusha is again called from the palace.* And finally the main question ...

GRUSHA: Simon Chachava, because I've got to go to the third courtyard and I'm in a hurry, the answer is 'Yes'.

SIMON *very embarrassed*: Hurry, they say, is the wind that blows down the scaffolding. But they also say: The rich don't know what hurry is. – I come from ...

GRUSHA: Kutsk.

SIMON: So the young lady has already made enquiries? Am healthy, have no dependents, earn ten piastres a month, as a paymaster twenty, and am asking honourably for your hand.

GRUSHA: Simon Chachava, that suits me.

SIMON *taking from his neck a thin chain from which hangs a little cross*: This cross belonged to my mother, Grusha Vachnadze. The chain is silver. Please wear it.

GRUSHA: I thank you, Simon. *He fastens it round her neck.*

SIMON: Now I must harness the horses. The young lady will understand that. It would be better for the young lady to go into the third courtyard. Otherwise there'll be trouble.

GRUSHA: Yes, Simon.

They stand together undecided.

SIMON: I'll just take the woman to the troops who've remained loyal. When the war's over, I'll come back. In two weeks. Or three. I hope my intended won't get tired waiting for my return.

GRUSHA: Simon Chachava, I shall wait for you.
      Go calmly into battle, soldier
      The bloody battle, the bitter battle
      From which not everyone returns.
      When you return I will be there.
      I will be waiting for you under the green elm
      I will be waiting for you under the bare elm
      I will wait until the last soldier has returned
      And even longer.
      When you return from the battle
      No boots will lie before the door
      The pillow beside mine will be empty
      My mouth will be unkissed.
      When you return, when you return
      You will be able to say: all is as it was.

SIMON: I thank you, Grusha Vachnadze, and farewell!

He bows low before her; she bows low before him. Then she runs off without looking round. Enter the Adjutant from the gateway.

THE ADJUTANT *harshly*: Harness the horses to the big carriage! Don't stand there doing nothing, idiot!

Simon Chachava leaps to attention and goes off. Two servants crawl in from the gateway, loaded down with heavy trunks. Behind them, supported by her women, stumbles Natella Abashvili. She is followed by another woman carrying Michael.

19

THE GOVERNOR'S WIFE: As usual, nobody's paying the slightest attention. I hardly know if I'm standing on my head or my feet. Where's Michael? Don't hold him so clumsily! Pile the trunks on to the carriage! Shalva, is there any news of the Governor?

THE ADJUTANT *shaking his head*: You must get away at once.

THE GOVERNOR'S WIFE: Is there any news from the town?

THE ADJUTANT: No. So far all is quiet. But there isn't a minute to lose. There's not enough room for the trunks on the carriage. Please pick out what you need.

Exit the Adjutant quickly.

THE GOVERNOR'S WIFE: Only essentials! Quick, open the trunks. I'll tell you what I've got to have.

The trunks are lowered and opened.

THE GOVERNOR'S WIFE *pointing at some brocade dresses*: That green one! And of course that one with the fur trimming. Where are the doctors? I'm getting this terrible migraine again. It always starts in the temples. This one with the little pearl buttons . . . *Enter Grusha.* You're taking your time, eh? Go and get the hot water bottles at once!

Grusha runs off, and returns with hot water bottles. The Governor's wife orders her about by signs.

THE GOVERNOR'S WIFE *watching a young woman attendant*: Don't tear the sleeve!

THE YOUNG WOMAN: I promise you, madam, no harm has come to the dress.

THE GOVERNOR'S WIFE: Because I caught you. I've been watching you for a long time. Nothing in your head but making eyes at the Adjutant. I'll kill you, you bitch! *She beats her.*

THE ADJUTANT *returning*: I must ask you to make haste, Natella Abashvili. They are fighting in the town. *Exit the Adjutant.*

THE GOVERNOR'S WIFE *letting go of the young woman*: My God, do you think they'll do something to me? Why should they? *All are silent. She herself begins to rummage in the trunks.* Where's my brocade jacket? Help me! What about Michael? Is he asleep?

THE NURSE: Yes, madam.

THE GOVERNOR'S WIFE: Then put him down a moment and go and fetch my little saffron-coloured slippers from the bed-chamber. I need them to go with the green dress. *The nurse puts down the child and goes off. To the young woman*: Don't stand around, you! *The young woman runs off.* Stay here, or I'll have you whipped! Just look at the way these things have been packed! No love! No understanding! If one doesn't give every order oneself . . . At such moments one realises what one's servants are like! Masha! *She gives her an order with a wave of the hand.* You all gorge yourselves, but never a sign of gratitude! I won't forget this.

THE ADJUTANT *very excited*: Natella, you must leave at once! Orbeliani, Judge of the Supreme Court, has just been hanged! The carpet weavers are in revolt!

THE GOVERNOR'S WIFE: Why? I must have the silver dress – it cost 1000 piastres. And that one there, and all my furs. And where's the wine-coloured dress?

THE ADJUTANT *trying to pull her away*: Riots have broken out in the outer town! We've got to leave this minute! *A servant runs off.* Where's the child?

THE GOVERNOR'S WIFE *to the nurse*: Maro, get the child ready! Where are you?

THE ADJUTANT *leaving*: We'll probably have to do without the carriage. And ride.

The Governor's wife still rummages among her dresses, throws some on to the heap to go with her, then takes them off again. Drums are heard. The sky begins to redden.

THE GOVERNOR'S WIFE *rummaging desperately*: I can't find that wine-coloured dress. *Shrugging her shoulders, to the second woman*: Take the whole heap and carry it to the carriage. Why hasn't Maro come back? Have you all gone off your heads? I told you it's right at the bottom.

THE ADJUTANT *returning*: Quick! Quick!

THE GOVERNOR'S WIFE *to the second woman*: Run! Just throw them into the carriage!

THE ADJUTANT: We're not going by carriage. Come at once or I'll ride off on my own!

THE GOVERNOR'S WIFE: Maro! Bring the child! *To the second woman*: Go and look, Masha. No, first take the dresses to the carriage. It's all nonsense, I wouldn't dream of riding! *Turning round, she sees the fire-reddened sky and starts back in horror.* Fire! *She rushes off, followed by the Adjutant. The second woman, shaking her head, follows with a heap of dresses. Servants enter from the gateway.*

THE COOK: That must be the East Gate that's burning.

THE CHEF: They've gone. And without the food wagon. How are we going to get away now?

A STABLEMAN: This is going to be an unhealthy place for some time. *To the third chambermaid*: Sulika, I'm going to fetch some blankets, we're clearing out.

THE NURSE *entering through the gateway with her mistress's slippers*: Madam!

A FAT WOMAN: She's gone.

THE NURSE: And the child. *She rushes to the child, and picks it up.* They left it behind, those brutes! *She hands the child to Grusha.* Hold it for a moment. *Deceitfully.* I'm going to look for the carriage.

She runs off, following the Governor's wife.

GRUSHA: What have they done to the Governor?

THE STABLEMAN *drawing his index finger across his throat*: Fft.

THE FAT WOMAN *seeing the gesture, becomes hysterical*: Oh God! Oh God! Oh God! Our master Georgi Abashvili! At morning Mass he was a picture of health! And now! Oh, take me away! We're all lost! We must die in sin! Like our master, Georgi Abashvili!

THE THIRD WOMAN *trying to calm her*: Calm down, Nina. You'll get away. You've done no one any harm.

THE FAT WOMAN *being led out*: Oh God! Oh God! Oh God! Let's all get out before they come! Before they come!

THE THIRD WOMAN: Nina takes it to heart more than the mistress. People like that get others even to do their *weeping* for them! *Seeing the child in Grusha's arms.* The child! What are you doing with it?

GRUSHA: It's been left behind.

THE THIRD WOMAN: She just left it? Michael, who was never allowed to be in a draught!

The servants gather round the child.

GRUSHA: He's waking up.

THE STABLEMAN: Better put him down, I tell you. I'd rather not think what'd happen to the person seen with that child. I'll get our things. You wait here.

Exit into the palace.

THE COOK: He's right. Once they begin, they'll slaughter whole families. I'll go and fetch my belongings.

All go except the cook, the third woman and Grusha with the child in her arms.

THE THIRD WOMAN: Didn't you hear? Better put him down!

GRUSHA: The nurse asked me to hold him for a moment.

THE COOK: That one won't come back, you silly!

THE THIRD WOMAN: Keep your hands off him.

THE COOK: They'll be more after him than after his mother. He's the heir. Grusha, you're a good soul. But you know you're not too bright. I tell you, if he had the plague it couldn't be worse. Better see to it that you get away.

The stableman has come back carrying bundles which he distributes among the women. They all prepare to leave except Grusha.

GRUSHA *stubbornly*: He hasn't got the plague. He looks at you like a human being.

THE COOK: Then don't you look back. You're just the kind of fool who always gets put upon. If someone says to you: Run and get the lettuce, you have the longest legs! – you run. We're taking the ox-cart, you can have a lift if you hurry. Jesus, by now the whole neighbourhood must be in flames!

THE THIRD WOMAN: Haven't you packed anything yet? There isn't much time, you know. The Ironshirts will soon be here from the barracks.

Exit both women and the stableman.

GRUSHA: I'm coming.

Grusha lays the child down, looks at it for a moment, then takes clothes from the trunks lying about and covers the sleeping child. Then she runs into the palace to get her things. Sounds of horses' hoofs and of women screaming. Enter the fat prince with drunken Ironshirts. One of them carries the head of the Governor on a lance.

THE FAT PRINCE: Put it here. Right in the middle! *One Ironshirt climbs on to the back of another, takes the head and holds it over the gateway.* That's not the middle. Further to the right. Good. What I do, my friends, I do well. *While an Ironshirt with hammer and nail fastens the head by its hair:* This morning at the church door I said to Georgi Abashvili: 'I love a clear sky'. Actually, what I prefer is lightning from a clear sky. Oh, yes. But it's a pity they took the brat away. . I need him. Badly. Search the whole of Grusinia for him! 1000 piastres reward!

As Grusha enters cautiously through the doorway, the fat prince and the Ironshirts leave. Trampling of horses' hoofs again. Carrying a bundle, Grusha walks towards the gateway. At the last moment, she turns to see if the child is still there. Promptly the singer begins to sing. She stands rooted to the spot.

THE SINGER:

> As she was standing between courtyard and gate, she heard
> Or thought she heard, a low voice. The child
> Called to her, not whining but calling quite sensibly
> At least so it seemed to her: 'Woman', it said, 'Help me'.
> Went on calling not whining but calling quite sensibly:
> 'Don't you know, woman, that she who does not listen to
>   a cry for help
> But passes by shutting her ears, will never hear
> The gentle call of a lover
> Nor the blackbird at dawn, nor the happy
> Sigh of the exhausted grape-picker at the sound of the
>   Angelus.
> Hearing this

Grusha walks a few steps towards the child and bends over it.

> she went back to the child
> Just for one more look, just to sit with it
> For a moment or two till someone should come
> Its mother, perhaps, or someone else –

She sits down opposite the child, and leans against a trunk.

> Just for a moment before she left, for now the danger was
>   too great
> The city full of flame and grief.

The light grows dimmer as though evening and night were falling,
Grusha has gone into the palace and fetched a lamp and some milk.
which she gives the child to drink.

THE SINGER *loudly*:
> Terrible is the temptation to do good!

Grusha now settles down to keep watch over the child through the
night. Once, she lights a small lamp to look at it. Once, she tucks it
in with a brocade coat. Now and again she listens and looks up to
see if someone is coming.

> For a long time she sat with the child.
> Evening came, night came, dawn came.
> Too long she sat, too long she watched
> The soft breathing, the little fists
> Till towards morning the temptation grew too strong.
> She rose, she leaned over, she sighed, she lifted the child
> She carried it off.

She does what the singer says as he describes it.

> Like booty she took it for herself
> Like a thief she sneaked away.

3

THE FLIGHT INTO THE NORTHERN MOUNTAINS

THE SINGER:

> As Grusha Vachnadze left the city
> On the Grusinian highway
> Towards the northern mountains
> She sang a song, she bought some milk.

THE MUSICIANS:

> How will the merciful escape the merciless
> The bloodhounds, the trappers?
> Into the deserted mountains she wandered
> Along the Grusinian highway she wandered
> She sang a song, she bought some milk.

Grusha Vachnadze continues on her way. On her back she carries the child in a sack, in one hand a bundle, in the other a big stick.

GRUSHA *singing*:

> Four generals set off for Iran
> Four generals but not one man.
> The first did not strike a blow
> The second did not beat the foe
> For the third the weather was not right
> For the fourth the soldiers would not fight.
> Four generals went forth to attack
> Four generals turned back.
>
> Sosso Robakidse marched to Iran
> Sosso Robakidse was a man.
> He struck a sturdy blow
> He certainly beat the foe
> For him the weather was good enough
> For him the soldiers fought with love
> Sosso Robakidse marched to Iran
> Sosso Robakidse is our man.

A peasant's cottage appears.

GRUSHA *to the child*: Noontime, eating time. Now we'll sit here quietly in the grass, while the good Grusha goes and buys a little mug of milk. *She lays the child down and knocks at the cottage door. An old peasant opens it.* Grandpa, could I have a little mug of milk? And perhaps a corn cake?

THE OLD MAN: Milk? We haven't any milk. The soldiers from the city took our goats. If you want milk, go to the soldiers.

GRUSHA: But Grandpa, you surely have a mug of milk for a child?

THE OLD MAN: And for a 'God Bless You', eh?

GRUSHA: Who said anything about a 'God Bless You'? *She pulls out her purse.* We're going to pay like princes. Head in the clouds, bottom in the water! *The peasant goes off grumbling to fetch milk.* And how much is this mug?

THE OLD MAN: Three piastres. Milk has gone up.

GRUSHA: Three piastres for that drop? *Without a word the old man slams the door in her face.* Michael, did you hear that? Three piastres! We can't afford that. *She goes back, sits down again and gives the child her breast.* Well, we must try again like this. Suck. Think of the three piastres. There's nothing there, but you think you're drinking, and that's something. *Shaking her head, she realises the child has stopped sucking. She gets up, walks back to the door, and knocks again.* Open, Grandpa, we'll pay. *Under her breath*: May God strike you! *When the old man appears again*: I thought it would be half a piastre. But the child must have something. What about one piastre?

THE OLD MAN: Two.

GRUSHA: Don't slam the door again. *She rummages a long time in her purse.* Here are two piastres. But this milk has got to last. We still have a long journey ahead of us. These are cut-throat prices. It's a sin.

THE OLD MAN: If you want milk, kill the soldiers.

GRUSHA *letting the child drink*: That's an expensive joke. Drink, Michael. This is half a week's pay. The people here think we've earned our money sitting on our bottom. Michael, Michael, I certainly took on a nice burden with you! *Looking at the brocade coat in which the child is wrapped*: A brocade

27

coat worth 1000 piastres, and not one piastre for milk. *She glances round.* Look! There's a carriage, with rich ladies. We ought to get on to that.

In front of a caravansary. Grusha dressed in the brocade coat is seen approaching two elegant ladies. She holds the child in her arms.

GRUSHA: Oh, the ladies want to spend the night here, too? It's awful how crowded it is everywhere! And not a carriage to be found! My coachman simply turned back. I've been walking half a mile on foot. Barefoot, too! My Persian shoes – you know those heels! But why doesn't someone come?

THE ELDER LADY: That innkeeper certainly takes his time. The whole country has lost its manners since those goings-on started in the capital.

The innkeeper appears, a very dignified old man with a long beard, followed by his servant.

THE INNKEEPER: Excuse an old man for keeping you waiting, ladies. My little grandchild was showing me a peach tree in blossom. There on the slope, beyond the cornfields. We're planting fruit trees there, a few cherries. Further west – *pointing* – the ground gets more stony. That's where the farmers graze their sheep. You ought to see the peach blossom, the pink is exquisite.

THE ELDER LADY: You live in a fertile region.

THE INNKEEPER: God has blessed it. How far on is the fruit-blossom further south, my ladies? I take it you come from the south?

THE YOUNGER LADY: I must admit I haven't been paying much attention to the landscape.

THE INNKEEPER *politely*: Of course, the dust. It is advisable to travel slowly on our high roads. Provided, of course, one isn't in too great a hurry.

THE ELDER LADY: Put your scarf round your throat, dearest. The evening breeze seems rather cool here.

THE INNKEEPER: It comes down from the Janga-Tau glaciers, my ladies.

GRUSHA: Yes, I'm afraid my son may catch cold.

THE ELDER LADY: A very spacious caravansary! Shall we go in?

THE INNKEEPER: Oh, the ladies want rooms? But the caravansary is full up, my ladies. And the servants have run off. I very much regret it, but I cannot accommodate another person, not even with references . . .

THE YOUNGER LADY: But we can't spend the night here on the road.

THE ELDER LADY *drily*: How much?

THE INNKEEPER: My ladies, you will understand that in these times, when so many fugitives, no doubt quite respectable people but not popular with the authorities, are looking for shelter, a house has to be particularly careful. Therefore . . .

THE ELDER LADY: My dear man, we aren't fugitives. We're simply moving to our summer residence in the mountains, that's all. It would never occur to us to ask for hospitality if we needed it – all that urgently.

THE INNKEEPER *nodding his head in agreement*: Of course not. I only doubt if the tiny room at my disposal would suit the ladies. I have to charge 60 piastres per person. Are the ladies together?

GRUSHA: In a way. I'm also in need of shelter.

THE YOUNGER LADY: 60 piastres! That's a cut-throat price.

THE INNKEEPER *coldly*: My ladies, I have no desire to cut throats. That's why . . . *He turns to go*.

THE ELDER LADY: Must we talk about throats? Let's go in.

She enters, followed by the servant.

THE YOUNGER LADY *desperate*: 180 piastres for one room! *Glancing back at Grusha*: But with the child it's impossible! What if it cries?

THE INNKEEPER: The room costs 180, whether it's two persons or three.

THE YOUNGER LADY *changing her attitude to Grusha*: On the other hand, I couldn't bear to think of you on the road, my dear. Do come in.

They enter the caravansary. From the rear on the opposite side of the stage the servant appears with some luggage. Behind him come the elder lady, the younger lady and Grusha with the child.

THE YOUNGER LADY: 180 piastres! I haven't been so upset since they brought dear Igor home.

THE ELDER LADY: Must you talk about Igor?

THE YOUNGER LADY: Actually, we are four persons. The child is one too, isn't it? *To Grusha*: Couldn't you pay half at least?

GRUSHA: That's impossible. I had to leave in a hurry, you see. And the Adjutant forgot to slip me enough money.

THE ELDER LADY: Perhaps you haven't even got the 60?

GRUSHA: That much I'll pay.

THE YOUNGER LADY: Where are the beds?

THE SERVANT: There aren't any beds. Here are some sacks and blankets. You'll have to arrange them yourselves. Be glad you're not being put in a hole in the earth. Like lots of others. *Exit.*

THE YOUNGER LADY: Did you hear that? I'm going straight to the innkeeper. That man must be whipped.

THE ELDER LADY: Like your husband?

THE YOUNGER LADY: Don't be so cruel! *She weeps.*

THE ELDER LADY: How are we going to arrange something to sleep on?

GRUSHA: I'll see to that. *She puts down the child.* It's always easier when there are several hands. You still have the carriage. *Sweeping the floor.* I was taken completely by surprise. 'My dear Anastasia Katarinovska,' my husband was saying before luncheon, 'do go and lie down for a while. You know how easily you get your migraine.' *She spreads out sacks and makes beds. The ladies, watching her work, exchange glances.* 'Georgi', said I to the Governor, 'I can't lie down when there are sixty for luncheon. And one can't trust the servants. And Michael Georgivich won't eat without me.' *To Michael*: See, Michael? Everything'll be all right, what did I tell you! *She suddenly realises that the ladies are watching her strangely and whispering.* Well, there we are! At least one doesn't have to lie on the bare floor. I've folded the blankets double.

THE ELDER LADY *imperiously*: You seem to be rather clever at making beds, my dear. Let's have a look at your hands!

GRUSHA *frightened*: What?

THE YOUNGER LADY: You're being asked to show your hands.

Grusha shows the ladies her hands.

THE YOUNGER LADY *triumphant*: Cracked! A servant!

THE ELDER LADY *goes to the door and shouts*: Service!

THE YOUNGER LADY: You're caught! You swindler! Just confess what mischief you're up to!

GRUSHA *confused*: I'm not up to any mischief. I just thought you might take us a little way in your carriage. Please, I ask you, don't make a noise, I'll go on my own.

THE YOUNGER LADY *while the elder lady continues shouting for service*: Yes, you'll go all right, but with the police. For the moment you'll stay. Don't you dare move, you!

GRUSHA: But I was ready to pay the 60 piastres. Here. *She shows her purse.* Look for yourself. I have them. Here are four tens, and here's a five – no, that's another ten, and ten, makes 60. All I want is to get the child on to the carriage. That's the truth.

THE YOUNGER LADY: Aha, so that's what you want. On to the carriage! Now it's come out.

GRUSHA: Madam, I confess, I am from a humble family. Please don't call the police. The child is of noble birth, look at the linen. It's fleeing, like you yourself.

THE YOUNGER LADY: Of noble birth! We know that one. The father's a prince, eh?

GRUSHA *to the elder lady, fiercely*: Stop shouting! Have you no heart at all?

THE YOUNGER LADY *to the elder lady*: Look out! She'll attack you! She's dangerous! Help! Murder!

THE SERVANT *entering*: What's going on here?

THE ELDER LADY: This person here has smuggled herself in by playing the lady. She's probably a thief.

THE YOUNGER LADY: And a dangerous one, too. She wanted to murder us. It's a case for the police. Oh God, I can feel my migraine coming on!

THE SERVANT: There aren't any police at the moment. *To Grusha*: Pack up your things, sister, and make yourself scarce.

GRUSHA *angrily picking up the child*: You monsters! And they're already nailing your heads to the wall!

THE SERVANT *pushing her out*: Shut your trap. Or you'll have the Old Man here. And there's no trifling with him.

THE ELDER LADY *to the younger lady*: Just see if she hasn't stolen something already!

While the ladies, right, look feverishly to see whether something has been stolen, the servant and Grusha go out through the door, left.

THE SERVANT: Look before you leap, I say. Another time have a good look at people before you get mixed up with them.

GRUSHA: I thought they'd be more likely to treat their own kind better.

THE SERVANT: Not them! Believe me, nothing's harder than aping a lazy useless person. Once they suspect you can wipe your own arse, or that your hands have ever touched a broom, the game's up. Just wait a minute, I'll get you a corn cake and a few apples.

GRUSHA: Better not. I must get out before the Old Man comes. And if I walk all night I'll be out of danger, I think.

She walks away.

THE SERVANT *calling after her in a low voice*: At the next cross-roads, turn right.

She disappears.

THE SINGER:
  As Grusha Vachnadze wandered northwards
  She was followed by the Prince's Ironshirts
THE MUSICIANS:
  How will the barefooted girl escape the Ironshirts
  The bloodhounds, the trappers?
  They are hunting even by night.
  Pursuers don't get tired.
  Butchers sleep little.

Two Ironshirts are trudging along the highway.

THE CORPORAL: Blockhead, you'll never amount to anything. Why? Because your heart's not in it. Your superior sees it in little things. Yesterday when I laid that fat woman, I admit you collared her husband as I commanded. And you did kick him in the stomach. But did you enjoy it like a good soldier? Or did you just do it from a sense of duty? I've kept my eyes on you, blockhead. You're like a hollow reed or a tinkling cymbal. You'll never get promoted. *They walk awhile in silence.* Don't you get the idea I don't notice how insubordinate you are in every way. I forbid you to limp! You do it simply because I sold the horses, and I sold them because I'd never have got that price again. I know you: you limp just to show me you don't like marching. But that won't help you. It'll go against you. Sing!

THE TWO IRONSHIRTS *singing*:

O sadly one morning, one morning in May
I kissed my darling and rode far away.
Protect her, dear friends, until home from the wars
I come riding in triumph, alive on my horse.

THE CORPORAL: Louder!

THE TWO IRONSHIRTS:

When I lie in my grave and my sword turns to rust
My darling shall bring me a handful of dust.
For the feet that so gaily ran up to her door
And the arms that went round her shall please her no more.

They begin to walk again in silence.

THE CORPORAL: A good soldier has his heart and soul in it. He lets himself be hacked to pieces by his superiors, and even while dying he's aware of his Corporal nodding approval. For him that's reward enough. That's all he wants. But *you* won't get a nod. And you'll croak just the same. Christ, how am I to lay my hands on the Governor's bastard with an ass like you!

They trudge on.

33

THE SINGER:

> When Grusha Vachnadze came to the River Sirra
> The flight grew too much for her, the helpless child too
> heavy.

THE MUSICIANS:

> The rosy dawn in the cornfields
> Is nothing but cold to the sleepless.
> The gay clatter of the milk cans in the farmyard
> Where the smoke rises is nothing but a threat to the
> fugitives.
> She who drags the child feels nothing but its weight.

Grusha stops in front of a farm.

GRUSHA: Now you've wetted yourself again, and you know I've no nappies. Michael, we've got to part. This is far enough from the city. They won't want you so badly, little squit, that they'll follow you all this way. The woman looks kind, and just you smell the milk! So farewell, little Michael. I'll forget how you kicked me in the back all night to make me go faster. And you – you forget the meagre fare. It was meant well. I'd love to have kept you, because your nose is so small, but it can't be done. I'd have shown you your first rabbit and – how not to wet yourself, but I must turn back, because my sweetheart the soldier might soon return, and suppose he didn't find me? You can't ask that of me, Michael.

A fat peasant woman carries a milk can to the door. Grusha waits until she has gone in, then gingerly approaches the house. She tiptoes to the door and lays the child on the threshold. Then, hiding behind a tree, she waits until the peasant woman opens the door and sees the bundle.

THE PEASANT WOMAN: Jesus Christ, what's this? Husband!
THE PEASANT: What's up? Let me have my soup.
THE PEASANT WOMAN *to the child*: Where's your mother? Haven't you got one? It's a boy. And the linen is fine; it's from a good family. And they just leave him on our doorstep. Oh, what times we live in!

THE PEASANT: If they think we're going to feed it, they're mistaken. You take it to the priest in the village. That's all we can do.

THE PEASANT WOMAN: What will the priest do with it? It needs a mother. There, it's waking up. Don't you think we could keep it?

THE PEASANT *shouting*: No!

THE PEASANT WOMAN: I could lay it in the corner, next to the armchair. I only need a crib for it. And I can take it into the fields with me. Look how it's smiling! Husband, we have a roof over our heads and we can do it. I won't hear another word.

She carries the child into the house. The peasant follows, protesting. Grusha steps out from behind the tree, laughs, and hurries away in the opposite direction.

THE SINGER: Why so gay, you, making for home?
THE MUSICIANS:
> Because with a smile the child
> Has won new parents for himself, that's why I'm gay.
> Because I am rid of the loved one
> That's why I'm happy.

THE SINGER: And why are you sad?
THE MUSICIANS:
> I'm sad because I'm single and free
> Of the little burden in whom a heart was beating:
> Like one robbed, like one impoverished I'm going.

Grusha walks for a short while, then meets the two Ironshirts, who hold her up at the point of a lance.

THE CORPORAL: Young lady, you're running into the Armed Forces. Where are you coming from? When are you coming? Are you entertaining illegal relations with the enemy? Where is he hiding? What sort of movements is he making in your rear? What about the hills? What about the valley? How are your stockings fastened?

Grusha stands there frightened.

35

GRUSHA: They are strongly fastened; you'd better withdraw.

THE CORPORAL: I always withdraw. In that respect I'm reliable. Why are you staring like that at the lance? In the field a soldier never loses control of his lance. That's an order. Learn it by heart, blockhead. Now then, young lady, where are you off to?

GRUSHA: To my intended, one Simon Chachava, of the Palace Guard in Nukha. Wait till I write to him; he'll break your bones for you.

THE CORPORAL: Simon Chachava? Indeed! I know him. He gave me the key, so I could keep an eye on you once in a while. Blockhead, we're getting unpopular. We must make her realise we have honourable intentions. Young lady, my apparent flippancy hides a serious nature. So I'll tell you officially: I want a child from you.

Grusha utters a little scream.

Blockhead, she has understood. Ooh, isn't that a sweet fright! 'But first I must take the bread out of the oven, Officer! But first I must change my torn chemise, Colonel!' But joking apart. Listen, young lady, we are looking for a certain child in these parts. Have you heard of a child from the city, of good family, dressed in fine linen?

GRUSHA: No, I've heard nothing.

THE SINGER:

Run, kind heart! The killers are coming!
Keep the helpless child, helpless girl! And so she runs.

Suddenly, panic-stricken, she turns round and runs. The Ironshirts glance at each other, then follow her, cursing.

THE MUSICIANS:

In the bloodiest times
There are still good people.

As Grusha enters the cottage, the peasant woman is bending over the child's crib.

GRUSHA: Hide it! Quick! The Ironshirts are coming! It was I

who laid it on your doorstep. But it isn't mine. It's of a noble family.

THE PEASANT WOMAN: Who's coming? What sort of Ironshirts?

GRUSHA: Don't ask questions. The Ironshirts who are looking for it.

THE PEASANT WOMAN: They've no business in my house. But it seems I must have a word with you.

GRUSHA: Take off the fine linen. That will give us away.

THE PEASANT WOMAN: Oh, you and your linen! In this house *I* decide. And don't you mess up my room. But why did you abandon it? That's a sin.

GRUSHA *looking out of the window*: There, they're coming from behind the trees. I shouldn't have run away. That gave them ideas. What on earth shall I do?

THE PEASANT WOMAN *looking out of the window and suddenly starting with fear*: Jesus and Mary! Ironshirts!

GRUSHA: They're after the child!

THE PEASANT WOMAN: But suppose they come in!

GRUSHA: You mustn't give it to them. Say it's yours.

THE PEASANT WOMAN: Yes.

GRUSHA: They'll run it through if you let them have it.

THE PEASANT WOMAN: But suppose they demand it? The money for the harvest is in the house.

GRUSHA: If you let them have it, they'll run it through, here in your room! You've got to say it's yours.

THE PEASANT WOMAN: Yes, but suppose they don't believe me?

GRUSHA: You must speak firmly.

THE PEASANT WOMAN: They'll burn the roof over our head.

GRUSHA: That's why you've got to say it's yours. His name's Michael. I shouldn't have told you that.

The peasant woman nods.

Don't nod your head like that. And don't tremble; they'll notice.

THE PEASANT WOMAN: Yes.

GRUSHA: Stop saying yes. I can't stand it any longer. *She shakes her.* Haven't *you* got a child?

37

THE PEASANT WOMAN *muttering*: In the war.

GRUSHA: Then perhaps he's an Ironshirt, too, by now? And what if he ran children through? You'd give him a fine piece of your mind! 'Stop waving that lance in my room! Is that what I've reared you for? Go and wash your neck before you speak to your mother.'

THE PEASANT WOMAN: That's true, I wouldn't let him behave like that.

GRUSHA: Promise me you'll say it's yours.

THE PEASANT WOMAN: Yes.

GRUSHA: There! They're coming!

There is a knocking at the door. The women don't answer. Enter the Ironshirts. The peasant woman bows deeply.

THE CORPORAL: Well, there she is. What did I tell you? My nose. I smelled her. Young lady, I have a question to ask you: Why did you run away? What did you think I would do to you? I'll bet it was something lewd. Confess!

GRUSHA *while the peasant woman continues to bow*: I'd left the milk on the stove. Then I suddenly remembered it.

THE CORPORAL: I thought it was because you imagined I'd looked at you in a lewd way – as if I were thinking there could be something between us. A lustful glance, know what I mean?

GRUSHA: I didn't see that.

THE CORPORAL: But it could have been, eh? You must admit that. After all, I could be a swine. I'm quite frank with you: I could think of all sorts of things if we were alone. *To the peasant woman*: Haven't you got something to do in the yard? The chickens to feed?

THE PEASANT WOMAN *falling suddenly to her knees*: Soldier, I didn't know anything about it. Please don't set my house on fire.

THE CORPORAL: What are you talking about?

THE PEASANT WOMAN: I have nothing to do with it. She left it on the doorstep, I swear.

THE CORPORAL *suddenly sees the child and whistles*: Ah, there's a

38

little one in the crib! Blockhead, I smell a thousand piastres.
Take the old girl out and hold on to her. It looks as though
I'll have to do some cross-examining.

*The peasant woman lets herself be led out by the soldier, without
a word.*

Well, there's the child I wanted to have from you. *He walks
towards the crib.*

GRUSHA: Officer, it's mine. It's not the one you're after.
THE CORPORAL: I'll just have a look at it. *He bends over the crib.
Grusha looks round in despair.*
GRUSHA: It's mine! It's mine!
THE CORPORAL: Nice linen!

*Grusha jumps at him to pull him away. He throws her off and again
bends over the crib. Looking round in despair, she suddenly sees a
big log of wood, seizes it in panic, and hits the Corporal over the
head from behind. She quickly picks up the child and dashes off.*

THE SINGER:
> After her escape from the Ironshirts
> After twenty-two days of wandering
> At the foot of the Janga-Tau glacier
> From this moment Grusha Vachnadze decided to be the
>   child's mother.

THE MUSICIANS:
> The helpless girl
> Became the mother of the helpless child.

*Grusha squats over a half-frozen stream to ladle some water in her
hand for the child.*

GRUSHA:
> Nobody wants to take you
> So I shall have to take you
> There is no-one else but me, my dear
> On this black day in a meagre year
> Who will not forsake you.

39

Since I've carried you too long
And with sore feet
Since the milk was too dear
I grew fond of you.
(I wouldn't be without you any more.)
I'll throw your fine little shirt away
And wrap you in rags
I'll wash you and christen you
With glacier water.
(You'll have to bear it.)

She has taken off the child's fine linen and wrapped it in a rag.

THE SINGER:

When Grusha Vachnadze, pursued by the Ironshirts
Came to the narrow footbridge on the Eastern slope
She sang the song of the rotten bridge
And risked two lives.

A wind has risen. The bridge on the glacier is visible in the semi-darkness. One rope is broken, and half the bridge is hanging down the precipice. Merchants, two men and a woman, stand undecided before the bridge as Grusha and the child arrive. One man is trying to retrieve a hanging rope with a stick.

THE FIRST MAN: Take your time, young woman. You won't get over that pass anyway.

GRUSHA: But I simply have to get my child over to the east side. To my brother.

THE MERCHANT WOMAN: Have to? What d'you mean by have to? I have to get there, too – because I have to buy two carpets in Atum – carpets a woman had to sell because her husband had to die. But can I do what I have to; can she? Andrei has been fishing for two hours for that rope. And I ask you, how are we to fasten it, even if he gets it?

THE FIRST MAN *listening*: Shush, I think I hear something.

GRUSHA: The bridge is not quite rotten. I think I'll try and cross it.

THE MERCHANT WOMAN: I wouldn't try that even if the devil himself were after me. It's suicide.

THE FIRST MAN *shouting*: Hi!

GRUSHA: Don't shout! *To the merchant woman*. Tell him not to shout.

THE FIRST MAN: But someone down there's calling. Perhaps they've lost their way.

THE MERCHANT WOMAN: And why shouldn't he shout? Is there something wrong with you? Are they after you?

GRUSHA: Well, I'll have to tell you. Ironshirts are after me. I knocked one down.

THE SECOND MAN: Hide our merchandise!

The woman hides a sack behind a rock.

THE FIRST MAN: Why didn't you tell us that at once? *To the other*: If they catch her they'll make mincemeat out of her!

GRUSHA: Get out of my way. I've got to cross that bridge.

THE SECOND MAN: You can't. There's a precipice of two thousand feet.

THE FIRST MAN: Even if we could get the rope it wouldn't make sense. We could hold it with our hands, but then the Ironshirts could get across in the same way.

GRUSHA: Out of my way.

Shouts from a distance: 'Let's get up there!'

THE MERCHANT WOMAN: They're getting near. But you can't take the child across that bridge. It's sure to break. Just look down!

Grusha looks down the precipice. The Ironshirts are heard shouting again from below.

THE SECOND MAN: Two thousand feet!

GRUSHA: But those men are worse.

THE FIRST MAN: Anyway you can't do it with the child. Risk your own life if they are after you, but not the child's.

THE SECOND MAN: She's even heavier with the child.

THE MERCHANT WOMAN: Perhaps she's really got to go. Give it to me. I'll hide it and you cross the bridge alone.

GRUSHA: I won't. We belong together. *To the child*: Live together, die together.

> If the gulf is deep
> And the rotten bridge sways
> It is not for us, son
> To choose our ways.

> The way that I know
> Is the one for your feet
> The bread that I find
> Is all you will eat.

> Of every four morsels
> You shall have three.
> I would that I knew
> How big they will be!

I'll try it.

THE MERCHANT WOMAN: That's tempting God.

Shouts from beneath.

GRUSHA: I beg you, throw that stick away, or they'll get the rope and follow me.

She starts off on to the swinging bridge. The merchant woman screams when the bridge looks like breaking. But Grusha walks on and reaches the far side.

THE FIRST MAN: She's done it!

THE MERCHANT WOMAN *who has fallen on her knees and begun to pray, angrily*: But I still think it was a sin.

The Ironshirts appear, the Corporal's head bandaged.

THE CORPORAL: Have you seen a woman with a child?

THE FIRST MAN *while the second throws away his stick*: Yes, there she is! But the bridge won't carry you!

THE CORPORAL: Blockhead, you'll suffer for this!

Grusha, from the far bank, laughs and shows the child to the Ironshirts. She walks on. The bridge is left behind. Wind.

GRUSHA *to the child*: You mustn't mind the wind. It's only a poor wretch, too. It has to push the clouds, and it feels the cold more than any of us. *Snow starts falling*. And the snow isn't the worst, Michael. It covers the little fir trees, so that they won't die in winter. And now I'll sing you a little song. Listen!

She sings:

> Your father's a thief
> Your mother's a whore:
> All the nice people
> Will love you therefore.
>
> The son of the tiger
> Brings the foals their feed
> The snake-child milk
> To mothers in need.

4

IN THE NORTHERN MOUNTAINS

THE SINGER:

> Seven days the sister wandered.
> Across the glacier, down the hills she wandered.
> 'When I enter my brother's house', she thought to herself
> 'He will rise and embrace me'.
> 'Is that you, sister?' he will say
> 'I have been expecting you for so long. This here is my
>   dear wife.
> And this is my farm, come to me by marriage.
> With eleven horses and thirty-one cows. Sit down.
> Sit down with your child at our table and eat.'
> The brother's house was in a lovely valley.
> When the sister came to the brother she was ill from her
>   wanderings.
> The brother rose from the table.

A fat peasant couple who have just sat down to a meal. Lavrenti

43

Vachnadze already has a napkin round his neck, as Grusha, pale and supported by a stableman, enters with the child.

LAVRENTI: Where do you come from, Grusha?

GRUSHA *feebly*: I've walked across the Janga-Tau Pass, Lavrenti.

STABLEMAN: I found her in front of the hay barn. She has a child with her.

THE SISTER-IN-LAW: Go and groom the roan. *Exit stableman.*

LAVRENTI: This is my wife, Aniko.

THE SISTER-IN-LAW: We thought you were in service in Nukha.

GRUSHA *barely able to stand*: Yes, I was there.

THE SISTER-IN-LAW: Wasn't it a good job? We were told it was a good one.

GRUSHA: The Governor has been killed.

LAVRENTI: Yes, we heard there were riots. Your aunt told us about it. Remember, Aniko?

THE SISTER-IN-LAW: Here, with us, it's quiet. City people always need some kind of excitement. *She walks towards the door and shouts*: Sosso, Sosso, take the flat cake out of the oven, d'you hear? Where are you? *Exit, shouting.*

LAVRENTI *quietly, quickly*: Has it got a father? *As she shakes her head*: I thought so. We must think up something. She's very pious.

THE SISTER-IN-LAW *returning*: These servants! *To Grusha*: You have a child?

GRUSHA: It's mine. *She collapses. Lavrenti helps her up.*

THE SISTER-IN-LAW: Mary and Joseph, she's ill – what are we to do?

Lavrenti tries to lead Grusha to the bench by the stove. Aniko waves her away in horror and points to the sack by the wall.

LAVRENTI *escorting her to the wall*: Sit down, sit down. I think it's just weakness.

THE SISTER-IN-LAW: As long as it's not scarlet fever.

LAVRENTI: Then she'd have spots. I'm sure it's only weakness. Don't worry, Aniko. *To Grusha*: Do you feel better sitting?

THE SISTER-IN-LAW: Is the child hers?

GRUSHA: It's mine.

44

LAVRENTI: She's on her way to her husband.

THE SISTER-IN-LAW: Really? Your meat's getting cold. *Lavrenti sits down and begins to eat.* Cold food's not good for you. At least the fat parts mustn't get cold; you know your stomach's your weak spot. *To Grusha:* If your husband's not in town, where is he then?

LAVRENTI: She got married on the other side of the mountain, she says.

THE SISTER-IN-LAW: Oh, on the other side! *She also sits down to eat.*

GRUSHA: I think I'll have to lie down somewhere, Lavrenti.

THE SISTER-IN-LAW *goes on questioning her:* If it's consumption we'll all get it. Has your husband a farm?

GRUSHA: He's a soldier.

LAVRENTI: But he's coming into a farm – a small farm from his father.

THE SISTER-IN-LAW: Isn't he in the war? Why not?

GRUSHA *wearily:* Yes, he's in the war.

THE SISTER-IN-LAW: Then why d'you want to go to the farm?

LAVRENTI: When he comes back from the war, he'll come to his farm.

THE SISTER-IN-LAW: But you're going there now?

LAVRENTI: Yes, to wait for him.

THE SISTER-IN-LAW *shrilly:* Sosso, the cake!

GRUSHA *murmurs in fever:* A farm – a soldier – waiting – sit down – eat.

THE SISTER-IN-LAW: That's scarlet fever.

GRUSHA *starting up:* Yes, he has a farm!

LAVRENTI: I think it must be weakness, Aniko. Wouldn't you like to go and look after the cake yourself, my dear?

THE SISTER-IN-LAW: But when will he come back if the war, as they say, has broken out again? *Waddling away, shouting:* Sosso! Where are you? Sosso!

LAVRENTI *getting up quickly and going to Grusha:* You'll get a bed in a moment. She has a good heart. But only after supper.

GRUSHA *holding out the child to him:* Take it. *He takes it, looking anxiously round.*

LAVRENTI: But you can't stay here long. You must realise she's very pious.

Grusha collapses. Lavrenti takes hold of her.

THE SINGER:

> The sister was too ill.
> The cowardly brother had to give her shelter.
> The autumn passed, the winter came.
> The winter was long
> The winter was short.
> The people mustn't know
> The rats mustn't bite
> The spring mustn't come.

Grusha sits bent at the weaving loom in the scullery. She and the child, who squats on the floor, are wrapped in blankets.

GRUSHA *sings while weaving*:

> Then the lover started to leave
> Then his girl ran pleading after him
> Pleading and crying, crying and pleading:
> Dearest mine, dearest mine
> As you now go into battle
> As you now have to fight the enemy
> Don't throw yourself into the front line
> And don't push with the rear line.
> In front is red fire
> In the rear is red smoke.
> Stay wisely in between
> Keep near the standard bearer.
> The first ones always die
> The last ones are also hit
> Those in the centre come home.

Michael, we must be clever. If we make ourselves really small, like cockroaches, the sister-in-law will forget we're in the house. Then we can stay here till the snow melts. And don't cry because of the cold. Being poor and cold as well puts people off.

Enter Lavrenti. He sits down beside Grusha.

LAVRENTI: Why are you two sitting there muffled up like coach-men? Perhaps it's too cold in the room?

GRUSHA *hastily removing her shawl*: It's not too cold, Lavrenti.

LAVRENTI: If it's too cold, you oughtn't to sit here with the child. Aniko would blame herself. *Pause.* I hope the priest didn't question you about the child.

GRUSHA: He did, but I didn't tell him anything.

LAVRENTI: That's good. I wanted to talk to you about Aniko. She has a good heart – but she's very, very sensitive. People only have to mention our farm and she's worried. She takes everything to heart, you know. Our milkmaid once went to church with a hole in her stocking. Ever since then my dear Aniko has always worn two pairs of stockings to church. It's hard to believe, but it's the old family in her. *He listens.* Are you sure there are no rats here? If so, you couldn't stay here. *Sounds of drops from the roof.* What's that dripping?

GRUSHA: Must be a barrel leaking.

LAVRENTI: Yes, it must be a barrel. Now you've already been here six months, haven't you? Was I talking about Aniko? Of course I didn't mention the Ironshirt. She has a weak heart. That's why she doesn't know you can't look for work. And that's why she made those remarks yesterday. *They listen again to the melting snow.* Can you believe it? She's worrying about your soldier. 'Suppose he comes back and doesn't find her!' she says, and lies awake. 'He can't come before the spring,' I tell her. The dear woman! *The drops begin to fall faster.* When d'you think he'll come? What's your idea? *Grusha is silent.* Not before the spring. That's what you think, too? *Grusha is silent.* I see you no longer believe he'll come back. *Grusha does not answer.* But when spring comes and the snow is melting on the passes you must leave here. Because then they can come and look for you. People are already talking about a child with an unmarried mother.

The beat of the falling drops has grown faster and steadier.

Grusha, the snow is melting on the roof and spring is here.

GRUSHA: Yes.

47

LAVRENTI *eagerly*: Let me tell you what we'll do. You need a place to go to. And because of the child – *he sighs* – you must have a husband, to stop people talking. I've made cautious enquiries about how we can get a husband for you, Grusha, and I've found one. I talked to a woman who has a son, just over the mountain, a little farm. She's willing.

GRUSHA: But I can't marry another man! I must wait for Simon Chachava.

LAVRENTI: Of course. That's all been considered. You don't need a man in bed, but a man on paper. And that's the very man I've found. The son of the woman I spoke to is dying. Isn't that wonderful? He's just at his last gasp. And everything's as we have said: A man just over the mountain! And when you reached him he died, and so you're a widow. What do you say?

GRUSHA: I could do with a document with seals for Michael.

LAVRENTI: A seal makes all the difference. Without a seal even the Shah of Persia couldn't prove he is the Shah. And you'll have a roof over your head.

GRUSHA: How much does she want for it?

LAVRENTI: 400 piastres.

GRUSHA: Where will you find the money?

LAVRENTI *guiltily*: Aniko's milk money.

GRUSHA: No-one will know us over there. I'll do it.

LAVRENTI *gets up*: I'll tell the woman at once. *Exit quickly*.

GRUSHA: Michael, you cause a lot of trouble. I came by you as the pear tree comes by the sparrows. And because a Christian bends down and picks up a crust of bread so it won't go to waste. Michael, I ought to have walked away quickly on that Easter Sunday in Nukha. Now I'm the fool.

THE SINGER:

> The bridegroom was lying on his deathbed, when the bride arrived.
>
> The bridegroom's mother was waiting at the door, bidding them hurry.
>
> The bride brought along a child, the witness hid it during the wedding.

48

A space divided by a partition. On one side a bed. Under the mosquito net lies a very sick man. On the other side the mother-in-law rushes in pulling Grusha after her. They are followed by Lavrenti and the child.

THE MOTHER-IN-LAW: Quick! Quick! Or he'll die on us before the wedding. *To Lavrenti*: But I was never told she already had a child.

LAVRENTI: What's it matter? *Pointing towards the dying man*: It's all the same to him in his condition.

THE MOTHER-IN-LAW: Him? But I won't survive the shame. We're honest people. *She begins to weep.* My Yussup doesn't have to marry someone who already has a child.

LAVRENTI: All right, I'll add another 200 piastres. You have it in writing that the farm will go to you; but she has the right to live here for two years.

THE MOTHER-IN-LAW *drying her tears*: It will hardly cover the funeral expenses. I hope she will really lend me a hand with the work. And now what's happened to the monk? He must have slipped out by the kitchen window. When they get wind in the village that Yussup's end is near, they'll all be round our necks. Oh dear! I'll go and get the monk. But he mustn't see the child.

LAVRENTI: I'll take care he doesn't see it. But why a monk? Why not a priest?

THE MOTHER-IN-LAW: Oh, he's just as good. I made one mistake: I paid him half his fee in advance. Now he'll have gone to the tavern. I hope . . . *She runs off*.

LAVRENTI: She saved on the priest, the wretch! She's hired a cheap monk.

GRUSHA: Send Simon Chachava to me if he turns up.

LAVRENTI: Yes. *Glancing at the sick man*: Won't you have a look at him?

Grusha, taking Michael to her, shakes her head.

He's not moving an eyelid. I hope we aren't too late.

They listen. On the opposite side enter neighbours, who look round and take up positions against the walls. They start muttering prayers. Enter the mother-in-law with the monk.

THE MOTHER-IN-LAW *surprised and angry, to the monk*: Now we're for it! *She bows to the guests.* I must ask you to wait a few moments. My son's bride has just arrived from town and we've got to have an emergency wedding. *She goes with the monk into the bedchamber.* I knew you'd spread it about. *To Grusha*: The wedding can start at once. Here's the licence. I and the bride's brother – *Lavrenti tries to hide in the background, after having quickly taken Michael away from Grusha. The mother-in-law beckons him away from the child –* the bride's brother and I are the witnesses.

Grusha has bowed to the monk. They approach the bed: the mother-in-law lifts the mosquito-net: the monk begins babbling the marriage service in Latin. Meanwhile the mother-in-law beckons to Lavrenti to get rid of the child, but Lavrenti, fearing that the child will cry, draws its attention to the ceremony. Grusha glances once at the child, and Lavrenti, holding the child's hand, waves a greeting.

THE MONK: Are you prepared to be a faithful, obedient and good wife to this man? And to cleave to him until death you do part?

GRUSHA *looking at the child*: Yes.

THE MONK *to the dying man*: And are you prepared to be a good and loving husband to your wife until death you do part?

As the dying man does not answer, the monk repeats the question, then looks round.

THE MOTHER-IN-LAW: Of course he is! Didn't you hear him say yes?

THE MONK: All right. We declare this marriage contracted. Now what about Extreme Unction?

THE MOTHER-IN-LAW: Nothing doing! The wedding was quite expensive enough. I must now take care of the mourners. *To Lavrenti*: Did we say 700?

LAVRENTI: 600. *He pays.* Now I don't want to sit and get acquainted with the guests. So farewell, Grusha. And if my widowed sister comes to visit me one day, she'll get a 'welcome' from my wife. Or I'll get disagreeable.

He leaves. The mourners glance after him without interest.

THE MONK: And may one ask whose this child is?

THE MOTHER-IN-LAW: Is there a child? I don't see any child.
And you don't see one either – understand? Or else I've seen
all kinds of things happening behind the tavern! Come along
now.

*They move back to the room. After Grusha has put down the child
and told it to be quiet, she is introduced to the neighbours.*

This is my daughter-in-law. She arrived just in time to find
dear Yussup still alive.

ONE OF THE WOMEN: He's been ill now a whole year, hasn't he?
When my Vassili was called up he was there to say goodbye.

ANOTHER WOMAN: Such things are terrible for a farm. With the
corn ripe on the stalk and the farmer in bed! It will be a
blessing for him if he doesn't suffer much longer, I say.

FIRST WOMAN *confidentially*: At first we thought he took to his
bed because of military service, you know. And now his end
is coming.

THE MOTHER-IN-LAW: Please sit down and have some cakes.

*She beckons to Grusha and both women go into the bedroom, where
they pick up trays of cakes from the floor. The guests, among them
the monk, sit on the floor and begin conversing in subdued voices.*

A VERY OLD PEASANT *to whom the monk has slipped the bottle he
has taken from his cassock*: There's a little one, you say! How
can Yussup have managed that?

THIRD WOMAN: Anyway, she was lucky to have brought it off
in time, with him so sick.

THE MOTHER-IN-LAW: They are gossiping already. And stuffing
themselves with the funeral cakes at the same time. And if
he doesn't die today, I'll have to bake fresh ones tomorrow.

GRUSHA: I'll bake them.

THE MOTHER-IN-LAW: When some riders passed by last night,

and I went out to see who they were, he was lying there like a corpse! That's why I sent for you. It can't take much longer. *She listens.*

THE MONK: Dear wedding guests and mourners! We stand deeply moved in front of a bed of death and marriage, because the bride gets into bed and the groom into the grave. The groom is already washed, and the bride is already hot. For in the marriage-bed lies the last Will, and that makes people randy. Oh, my children, how varied is the fate of man! The one dies to get a roof over his head, and the other marries so that flesh may be turned to dust, from which it was made. Amen.

THE MOTHER-IN-LAW *who has listened*: He's got his own back. I shouldn't have hired such a cheap one. That's what you'd expect. An expensive one knows how to behave. In Sura there's one who is even in the odour of sanctity; but of course he charges a fortune. A fifty-piastre priest like this one here has no dignity. And as for piety, he has precisely fifty piastres' worth, and no more. And when I fetched him from the tavern he was just finishing a speech and shouting: 'The war is over, beware of the peace!' We must go in.

GRUSHA *giving Michael a cake*: Eat this cake and be a good boy, Michael. We are respectable now.

The two women carry the trays of cakes to the guests. The dying man is sitting up in bed; he puts his head out from under the mosquito-net and watches the two women. Then he sinks back again. The monk takes two bottles from his cassock and offers them to the peasant beside him. Enter three musicians, to whom the monk waves with a grin.

THE MOTHER-IN-LAW *to the musicians*: What have you got your instruments for?

A MUSICIAN: Brother Anastasius here – *pointing at the monk* – told us there was a wedding going on.

THE MOTHER-IN-LAW: What! You brought them? Three more on my neck! Don't you know there's a dying man next door?

THE MONK: That's a tempting task for an artist. They could play a hushed Wedding March or a gay Funeral Dance.

THE MOTHER-IN-LAW: Well, you might as well play. I can't stop you eating, in any case.

The musicians play a musical medley. The women offer cakes.

THE MONK: The trumpet sounds like a whining baby. And you, little drum, what gossip are you spreading abroad?

A PEASANT *beside the monk*: What about the bride shaking a leg?

THE MONK: Shake the legs or rattle the bones?

THE PEASANT *beside the monk, singing*:

When pretty Miss Plushbottom wed
A rich man with no teeth in his head
They enquired, 'Is it fun?'
She replied, 'No, it's none.
Still, there're candles and soon he'll be dead.'

The mother-in-law throws the drunken man out. The music stops. The guests are embarrassed. Pause.

THE GUESTS *loudly*: Have you heard the latest? The Grand Duke's back! – But the Princes are against him. – Oh, the Shah of Persia, they say, has lent him a great army, to restore order in Grusinia. – How is this possible? After all, the Shah of Persia is against the Grand Duke! – But against disorder, too. – In any case, the war's over. Our soldiers are already coming back.

Grusha drops the tray of cakes.

AN OLD WOMAN *to Grusha*: Are you feeling ill? That's just excitement about dear Yussup. Sit down and rest awhile, my dear.

Grusha stands, swaying.

THE GUESTS: Now everything will be as it was. Only the taxes will go up because we'll have to pay for the war.

GRUSHA *weakly*: Did someone say the soldiers are back?

A MAN: I did.

GRUSHA: That can't be true.

THE MAN *to a woman*: Show her the shawl. We bought it from a soldier. It's from Persia.

GRUSHA *looking at the shawl*: They are here.

A long pause. Grusha kneels as if to pick up the cakes. As she does so she takes the silver cross and chain out of her blouse, kisses it, and starts praying.

THE MOTHER-IN-LAW *while the guests silently watch Grusha*: What's the matter with you? Won't you look after our guests? What's all this nonsense from the city got to do with us?

THE GUESTS *resuming their conversation while Grusha remains with her forehead bent to the ground*: Persian saddles can be bought from soldiers, but some exchange them for crutches. – Wars are won on one side only by the bigwigs, the soldiers on both sides are the losers. – At least the war's over now. It's something that they can't call you up any more. – *The dying man sits bolt upright in bed. He listens.* – What we need most are two weeks of good weather. – There's hardly a pear on our trees this year.

THE MOTHER-IN-LAW *offering the cakes*: Have some more cake. And enjoy it. There's more to come.

The mother-in-law goes to the bedroom with empty trays. Unaware of the dying man, she bends down to pick up some more cakes, when he begins to talk in a hoarse voice.

YUSSUP: How many more cakes are you going to stuff down their throats? D'you think I can shit money? *The mother-in-law starts, and stares at him aghast, while he puts his head out from behind the mosquito-net.* Did they say the war was over?

FIRST WOMAN *talking kindly to Grusha in the next room*: Has the young woman someone in the war?

THE MAN: That's good news that they're on their way home, eh?

YUSSUP: Don't stare so! Where's the wife you've foisted on me?

Receiving no answer, he climbs out of bed and in his nightshirt staggers past his mother into the other room. Trembling, she follows him with the cake tray.

THE GUESTS *seeing him and shrieking*: Jesus, Mary and Joseph! Yussup!

Everyone leaps up in alarm. The women rush to the door. Grusha, still on her knees, turns round and stares at the man.

54

YUSSUP: The funeral supper! That's what you'd like! Get out before I kick you out!

The guests stampede from the house.

YUSSUP *grumpily to Grusha*: That puts a spoke in your wheel, eh?

Receiving no answer, he turns round and takes a cake from the tray which his mother holds.

THE SINGER:

> Oh, confusion! The wife discovers that she has a husband!
> By day there's the child, by night there's the man.
> The lover is on his way day and night.
> The married couple are looking at each other. The chamber is narrow.

Yussup sits naked in a high wooden bathtub. His mother pours water from a jug. Next door in the bedroom Grusha cowers with Michael, who is playing at mending a straw mat.

YUSSUP: That's her business, not yours. Where's she hiding now?
THE MOTHER-IN-LAW *calling*: Grusha! The peasant wants you!
GRUSHA *to Michael*: There are still two holes to mend.
YUSSUP *as Grusha enters*: Scrub my back!
GRUSHA: Can't the peasant do that himself?
YUSSUP: 'Can't the peasant do that himself?' Get the brush!
   To hell with you! Are you the wife or are you a stranger?
   To the mother-in-law: Too cold!
THE MOTHER-IN-LAW: I'll run and get some more hot water.
GRUSHA: Let me do it.
YUSSUP: You stay here. *The mother-in-law goes out.* Rub harder.
   And don't make such a fuss. You've seen a naked man before.
   That child of yours can't have come out of thin air.
GRUSHA: The child was not conceived in joy, if that's what the peasant means.
YUSSUP *turning and grinning*: You don't look like that. *Grusha stops scrubbing him and starts back. Enter the mother-in-law.* This is a nice thing you've saddled me with here! A mule for a wife!

THE MOTHER-IN-LAW: She isn't willing.

YUSSUP: Pour – but go easy! Ow! Go easy, I said. *To Grusha.*
I'd be surprised if you hadn't been up to something in the
city. What else would you be here for? But I won't say anything about that. I also haven't said anything about the bastard you brought into my house. But my patience with you
is coming to an end. That's against nature. *To the mother-in-
law*: More! *To Grusha*: And even if your soldier does return,
you're married.

GRUSHA: Yes.

YUSSUP: But your soldier won't return now. Don't you believe it.

GRUSHA: No.

YUSSUP: You're cheating me. You're my wife and you're not my
wife. Where you lie, nothing lies. And yet no other woman
can lie there. When I go to work in the mornings I'm dead-
tired. When I lie down at night I'm awake as the devil. God
has made you a woman, and what d'you do about it? My
fields don't bring me in enough to buy myself a woman in
town. Besides, it's a long way. Woman hoes the fields and
parts her legs. That's what our calendar says. D'you hear?

GRUSHA: Yes. *Quietly.* I don't mean to cheat you out of it.

YUSSUP: She doesn't mean to! Pour some more water. *The
mother-in-law pours.* Ow!

THE SINGER:

> As she sat by the stream to wash the linen
> She saw his image in the water, and his face grew dimmer
> As the months passed by.
> As she raised herself to wring the linen
> She heard his voice from the murmuring maple, and his
> voice grew fainter
> As the months passed by.
> Prayers and sighs grew more numerous, tears and sweat
> flowed faster
> As the months passed by, as the child grew up.

*Grusha sits by a stream dipping linen into the water. Some distance
away a few children are standing. Grusha is talking to Michael.*

GRUSHA: You can play with them, Michael. But don't let them order you about because you're the smallest.

Michael nods and joins the children. They start playing.

THE TALLEST BOY: Today we're going to play Heads-off. *To a fat boy*: You're the Prince and you must laugh. *To Michael*: You're the Governor. *To a girl*: You're the Governor's wife and you cry when his head's chopped off. And I do the chopping. *He shows his wooden sword.* With this. First, the Governor's led into the courtyard. The Prince walks ahead. The Governor's wife comes last.

They form a procession. The fat boy goes ahead, and laughs. Then comes Michael, and the tallest boy, and then the girl, who weeps.

MICHAEL *standing still*: Me too chop head off!
THE TALLEST BOY: That's my job. You're the smallest. The Governor's part is easiest. All you do is kneel down and have your head chopped off. That's simple.
MICHAEL: Me too have sword.
THE TALLEST BOY: That's mine.

He gives him a kick.

THE GIRL *shouting to Grusha*: He doesn't want to do what he's told.
GRUSHA *laughing*: Even ducklings take to water, they say.
THE TALLEST BOY: You can play the Prince if you know how to laugh.

Michael shakes his head.

THE FAT BOY: I'm the best laugher. Let him chop off the head just once. Then you do it, then me.

Reluctantly the tallest boy hands Michael the wooden sword and kneels. The fat boy sits down, smacks his thigh and laughs with all his might. The girl weeps loudly. Michael swings the big sword and chops off the head. In doing so, he topples over.

THE TALLEST BOY: Hi, I'll show you how to do it properly.

Michael runs away, and the children run after him. Grusha laughs, following them with her eyes. On turning round, she sees Simon Chachava standing on the opposite bank. He wears a shabby uniform.

GRUSHA: Simon!

SIMON: Is that Grusha Vachnadze?

GRUSHA: Simon!

SIMON *politely*: A good morning, and good health to the young lady.

GRUSHA *gets up gaily and bows deeply*: A good morning to the soldier. And thank God he has returned in good health.

SIMON: They found better fish than me, so they didn't eat me, said the haddock.

GRUSHA: Courage, said the kitchen boy. Luck, said the hero.

SIMON: And how are things here? Was the winter bearable? Did the neighbour behave?

GRUSHA: The winter was a little rough, the neighbour as usual, Simon.

SIMON: May one ask if a certain person is still in the habit of putting her leg in the water when washing her linen?

GRUSHA: The answer is no. Because of the eyes in the bushes.

SIMON: The young lady is talking about soldiers. Here stands a paymaster.

GRUSHA: Is that worth twenty piastres?

SIMON: And board.

GRUSHA *with tears in her eyes*: Behind the barracks under the date trees.

SIMON: Just there. I see someone has kept her eyes open.

GRUSHA: Someone has.

SIMON: And has not forgotten. *Grusha shakes her head.* And so the door is still on its hinges, as they say. *Grusha looks at him in silence and shakes her head again.* What's that mean? Is something wrong?

GRUSHA: Simon Chachava, I can never go back to Nukha. Something has happened.

SIMON: What has happened?

GRUSHA: It so happened that I knocked down an Ironshirt.

SIMON: Grusha Vachnadze will have had her reasons for that.

GRUSHA: Simon Chachava, my name is also no longer what it was.

SIMON *after a pause*: I don't understand that.

GRUSHA: When do women change their names, Simon? Let me explain it to you: Nothing stands between us. Everything between us has remained as it was. You've got to believe that.

SIMON: How can nothing stand between us and things be changed?

GRUSHA: How can I explain it to you? So fast and with the stream between us? Couldn't you cross that bridge?

SIMON: Perhaps it's no longer necessary.

GRUSHA: It's most necessary. Come over, Simon. Quick!

SIMON: Is the young lady saying that someone has come too late?

Grusha looks up at him in despair, her face streaming with tears. Simon stares before him. He picks up a piece of wood and starts cutting it.

THE SINGER:
> So many words are said, so many words are left unsaid.
> The soldier has come. Whence he comes he doesn't say.
> Hear what he thought but didn't say:
> The battle began at dawn, grew bloody at noon.
> The first fell before me, the second behind me, the third at my side.
> I trod on the first, I abandoned the second, the captain sabred the third.
> My one brother died by steel, my other brother died by smoke.
> My neck was burnt by fire, my hands froze in my gloves, my toes in my socks.
> For food I had aspen buds, for drink I had maple brew, for bed I had stones in water.

SIMON: I see a cap in the grass. Is there a little one already?

GRUSHA: There is, Simon. How could I hide it? But please don't let it worry you. It's not mine.

SIMON: They say: Once the wind begins to blow, it blows through every crack. The woman need say no more.

Grusha lowers her head and says no more.

THE SINGER:
> There was great yearning but there was no waiting.
> The oath is broken. Why was not disclosed.
> Hear what she thought, but didn't say:
> While you fought in the battle, soldier
> The bloody battle, the bitter battle
> I found a child who was helpless
> And hadn't the heart to do away with it.
> I had to care for what otherwise would have come to harm
> I had to bend down on the floor for breadcrumbs
> I had to tear myself to pieces for what was not mine
> But alien.
> Someone must be the helper.
> Because the little tree needs its water
> The little lamb loses its way when the herdsman is asleep
> And the bleating remains unheard.

SIMON: Give me back the cross I gave you. Or better, throw it in the stream.

He turns to go.

GRUSHA: Simon Chachava, don't go away. It isn't mine, it isn't mine! *She hears the children calling.* What is it, children?

VOICES: Soldiers have come! – They are taking Michael away!

Grusha stands aghast as two Ironshirts, with Michael between them, come towards her.

IRONSHIRT: Are you Grusha? *She nods.* Is that your child?

GRUSHA: Yes. *Simon goes off.* Simon!

IRONSHIRT: We have official orders to take this child, found in your charge, back to the city. There is suspicion that it is Michael Abashvili, son and heir of the late Governor Georgi Abashvili, and his wife, Natella Abashvili. Here is the document and the seal.

They lead the child away.

GRUSHA *running after them and shouting*: Leave it here, please!
It's mine!

THE SINGER:

> The Ironshirts took the child away, the precious child.
> The unhappy girl followed them to the city, the dangerous
> place.
> The real mother demanded the child back. The foster
> mother faced her trial.
> Who will try the case, on whom will the child be bestowed?
> Who will be the Judge? A good one, a bad one?
> The city was in flames. On the Judgment Seat sat Azdak.

5

THE STORY OF THE JUDGE

THE SINGER:

> Listen now to the story of the Judge:
> How he turned Judge, how he passed judgment, what
> kind of Judge he is.
> On the Easter Sunday of the great revolt, when the Grand
> Duke was overthrown
> And his Governor Abashvili, father of our child, lost his
> head
> The village clerk Azdak found a fugitive in the woods and
> hid him in his hut.

*Azdak, in rags and tipsy, helps a fugitive dressed as a beggar into
his hut.*

AZDAK: Don't snort. You're not a horse. And it won't do you
any good with the police if you run like a dirty nose in April.
Stop, I tell you. *He catches the fugitive, who has trotted into
the hut as though he would go through the walls.* Sit down and
feed: here's a piece of cheese. *From under some rags in a chest
he fishes out some cheese, and the fugitive greedily begins to eat.*

Haven't had anything for some time, eh? *The fugitive groans.* Why did you run so fast, you arse-hole? The police wouldn't even have seen you!

THE FUGITIVE: Had to.

AZDAK: Blue funk? *The fugitive stares, uncomprehending.* Got the squitters? Afraid? Don't slobber like a Grand Duke or a sow. I can't stand it. It's well-born stinkers we've got to put up with as God made them. Not the likes of you. I once heard of a Senior Judge who farted at a public dinner. Just to show his independence. Watching you eat like that really gives me the most awful ideas! Why don't you say something? *Sharply.* Let's have a look at your hand. Can't you hear? Show me your hand. *The fugitive slowly puts out his hand.* White! So you're no beggar at all! A fraud! A swindle on legs! And here am I hiding you from the police as though you were a decent human being! Why run like that if you're a landowner? Because that's what you are. Don't try to deny it. I see it in your guilty face. *He gets up.* Get out of here! *The fugitive looks uncertainly at him.* What are you waiting for, you peasant-flogger?

THE FUGITIVE: Am hunted. Ask for undivided attention. Make proposition.

AZDAK: What do you want to make? A proposition? Well, if that isn't the height of insolence! He making a proposition! The bitten man scratches his fingers bloody, and the leech makes a proposition. Get out, I tell you!

THE FUGITIVE: Understand point of view. Persuasion. Will pay 100,000 piastres for one night. How's that?

AZDAK: What? Do you think you can buy me? And for 100,000 piastres? A third-rate farm. Let's say 150,000. Got it?

THE FUGITIVE: Not on me, of course. Will be sent. Hope, don't doubt.

AZDAK: Doubt profoundly! Get out!

The fugitive gets up and trots to the door. A voice from off-stage.

VOICE: Azdak!

The fugitive turns, trots to the opposite corner and stands still.

62

AZDAK *shouting*: I'm not in. *He walks to the door*. Is that you spying around here again, Shauva?

POLICEMAN SHAUVA *outside, reproachfully*: You've snared another rabbit, Azdak. You promised me it wouldn't happen again.

AZDAK *severely*: Shauva, don't talk about things you don't understand. The rabbit is a dangerous and destructive animal. It devours plants, especially what they call weeds. So it must be exterminated.

SHAUVA: Azdak, don't be so hard on me. I'll lose my job if I don't arrest you. I know you have a good heart.

AZDAK: I *don't* have a good heart! How often am I to tell you I'm a man of intellect?

SHAUVA *slyly*: I know, Azdak. You're a superior person. You say so yourself. I'm a Christian and an ignoramus. So I ask you: if one of the Prince's rabbits is stolen, and I'm a policeman, what am I to do with the offender?

AZDAK: Shauva, Shauva, shame on you! There you stand asking me a question. Nothing is more tempting than a question. Suppose you were a woman – let's say Nunovna, that bad girl – and you showed me your thigh – Nunovna's thigh, that is – and you asked me: what shall I do with my thigh? It itches. Is she as innocent as she pretends? No. I catch a rabbit, you catch a man. Man is made in God's image. Not so a rabbit, you know that. I'm a rabbit-eater; but you're a man-eater, Shauva. And God will pass judgment on you. Shauva, go home and repent. No, stop! There's something ... *He looks at the fugitive, who stands trembling in the corner*. No, it's nothing after all. Go home and repent. *He slams the door behind Shauva. To the fugitive*: Now you're surprised, eh? Surprised I didn't hand you over? But I couldn't hand over even a bedbug to that beast of a policeman! It goes against my grain. Don't tremble at the sight of a policeman. So old and yet so cowardly! Finish your cheese, but eat it like a poor man, or else they'll still catch you. Do I even have to tell you how a poor man behaves? *He makes him sit down, and then gives him back the cheese. The box is the table.*

Put your elbows on the table, and now surround the plate with your arms as though you expected the cheese to be snatched from you at any moment. What right have you to be safe? Now hold the knife as if it were a small sickle; and don't look so greedily at your cheese, look at it mournfully – because it's already disappearing – like all good things. *Azdak watches him.* They're after you. That speaks in your favour. But how can I be sure they're not mistaken about you? In Tiflis they once hanged a landowner, a Turk. He could prove he quartered his peasants instead of merely cutting them in half, as is the custom. And he squeezed twice the usual amount of taxes out of them. His zeal was above all suspicion, and yet they hanged him like a common criminal. Why? Because he was a Turk – something he couldn't do much about. An injustice! He got on to the gallows like Pontius Pilate into the Creed. In a word, I don't trust you.

THE SINGER:

> Thus Azdak gave shelter to the old beggar
> Only to find out that he was that murderer, the Grand Duke.
> And he was ashamed of himself, he accused himself and ordered the policeman
> To take him to Nukha, to Court, to be judged.

In the Court of Justice three Ironshirts sit drinking. From a pillar hangs a man in judge's robes. Enter Azdak, in chains, dragging Shauva behind him.

AZDAK *shouting*: I have helped the Grand Duke, the Grand Thief, the Grand Murderer, to escape! In the name of Justice, I demand to be judged severely in a public trial!

THE FIRST IRONSHIRT: Who is this queer bird?

SHAUVA: That's our clerk, Azdak.

AZDAK: I am despicable, treacherous, branded! Tell them, flat-foot, how I insisted on being put in chains and brought to the capital. Because I sheltered the Grand Duke, the Grand Swindler, by mistake. As I realised only afterwards when I found this document in my hut. *The Ironshirts study the docu-*

64

ment. To Shauva: They can't read. Point out that the branded man is accusing himself. Tell them how I forced you to walk with me through half the night, to get everything cleared up.

SHAUVA: And all by threats. That wasn't nice of you, Azdak.

AZDAK: Shauva, shut your trap. You don't understand. A new age has come, which will thunder over you. You're finished. The police will be wiped out, pfft! Everything will be investigated, brought into the open. In future a man will prefer to give himself up. Why? Because he won't be able to escape the people. Tell them how I've been shouting all along Shoemaker Street! *He acts with expansive gestures, looking sideways at the Ironshirts.* 'Out of ignorance I let the Grand Swindler escape. Tear me to pieces, brothers!' So as to get in first.

THE FIRST IRONSHIRT: And what was their answer?

SHAUVA: They comforted him in Butcher Street, and laughed themselves sick in Shoemaker Street. That's all.

AZDAK: But here with you it's different, I know you're men of iron. Brothers, where is the Judge? I must be tried.

THE FIRST IRONSHIRT *pointing at the hanged man*: Here's the Judge. And stop 'brothering' us. That's rather a sore spot this evening.

AZDAK: 'Here's the Judge.' That's an answer never heard in Grusinia before. Citizens, where's His Excellency the Governor? *Pointing at the gallows*: Here's His Excellency, stranger. Where's the Chief Tax Collector? Where's the official Recruiting Officer? The Patriarch? The Chief of Police? Here, here, here – all here. Brothers, that's what I expected from you.

THE SECOND IRONSHIRT: Stop! What did you expect, you bird?

AZDAK: What happened in Persia, brothers. What happened there.

THE SECOND IRONSHIRT: And what did happen in Persia?

AZDAK: Forty years ago. Everyone hanged. Viziers, tax-collectors. My grandfather, a remarkable man, saw it all. For three whole days. Everywhere.

THE SECOND IRONSHIRT: And who reigned after the Vizier was hanged?

AZDAK: A peasant.

THE SECOND IRONSHIRT: And who commanded the army?

AZDAK: A soldier, soldier.

THE SECOND IRONSHIRT: And who paid the wages?

AZDAK: A dyer. A dyer paid the wages.

THE SECOND IRONSHIRT: Wasn't it a carpet weaver perhaps?

THE FIRST IRONSHIRT: And why did all this happen, Persian?

AZDAK: 'Why did all this happen?' Must there be a special reason? Why do you scratch yourself, brother? War! Too long a war! And no justice! My grandfather brought back a song that tells what it was all about. I and my friend the policeman will sing it for you. *To Shauva*: And hold on to the rope, that's part of it. *He sings, with Shauva holding the rope.*

> Why don't your sons bleed any longer, why don't our daughters weep any more?
>
> Why do only the calves in the slaughterhouse have any blood, why only willows on Lake Urmi tears?
>
> The Grand King must have a new province, the peasant must relinquish his savings.
>
> In order to capture the roof of the world, the cottage roofs have to be torn down.
>
> Our men are scattered in all directions, so that the great ones can eat at home.
>
> The soldiers kill each other, the marshals salute each other.
>
> The widow's tax money has to be fingered to see if it's good, the swords break.
>
> The battle has been lost, but the helmets have been paid for.
>
> Is that right? Is that right?

SHAUVA: Yes, yes, yes, yes, yes, that's right.

AZDAK: Do you want to hear the whole thing?

The first Ironshirt nods.

THE SECOND IRONSHIRT *to Shauva*: Did he teach you that song?

SHAUVA: Yes. Only my voice isn't good.

THE SECOND IRONSHIRT: No. *To Azdak*: Go on singing.

AZDAK: The second verse is about the peace. *He sings*:

> The offices are jammed, the officials are working in the streets.

The rivers overflow their banks and lay waste the fields.

Those incapable of letting down their own trousers rule countries.

Those who can't count up to four devour eight courses.

The corn farmers look round for buyers, but see only the starving.

The weavers go home from their looms in rags.

Is that right? Is that right?

SHAUVA: Yes, yes, yes, yes, yes, that's right.

AZDAK:

That's why our sons bleed no longer, our daughters weep no more.

That's why only the calves in the slaughterhouse have any blood.

And the willows in the morning on Lake Urmi have any tears.

THE FIRST IRONSHIRT *after a pause*: Are you going to sing that song here in town?

AZDAK: Of course. What's wrong with it?

THE FIRST IRONSHIRT: Do you see the sky getting red? *Turning round, Azdak sees the sky reddened by fire.* That's in the outer town. This morning when Prince Kazbeki had Governor Abashvili beheaded our carpet weavers also caught the 'Persian disease'. They asked if Prince Kazbeki isn't eating too many courses. And this afternoon they strung up the town judge. But we beat them to pulp for two piastres per weaver, you understand?

AZDAK *after a pause*: I understand.

He glances shyly round and, creeping away, sits down in a corner, his head in his hands.

THE FIRST IRONSHIRT *to the third, after they have all had a drink*: Just wait and see what'll happen next.

The first and second Ironshirts walk towards Azdak and block his exit.

SHAUVA: I don't think he's a really bad character, gentlemen.

67

He poaches a few chickens here and there, and perhaps an odd rabbit.

THE SECOND IRONSHIRT *approaching Azdak*: You've come here to fish in troubled waters, eh?

AZDAK *looking up*: I don't know why I've come here.

THE SECOND IRONSHIRT: Do you happen to be in with the carpet weavers? *Azdak shakes his head.* And what about this song?

AZDAK: From my grandfather. A stupid, ignorant man.

THE SECOND IRONSHIRT: Right. And what about the dyer who paid the wages?

AZDAK: That was in Persia.

THE FIRST IRONSHIRT: And what about denouncing yourself for not having hanged the Grand Duke with your own hands?

AZDAK: Didn't I tell you that I let him escape?

SHAUVA: I swear to it. He let him escape.

The Ironshirts drag Azdak screaming to the gallows. Then they let him loose and burst out laughing. Azdak joins in the laughter, laughing loudest. They then unchain him. They all start drinking. Enter the fat prince with a young man.

THE FIRST IRONSHIRT *to Azdak*: There you have your new age.

More laughter.

THE FAT PRINCE: And what is there to laugh about here, me friends? Permit me a serious word. Yesterday morning thy Princes of Grusinia overthrew the Grand Duke's war-thirsty government and did away with his governors. Unfortunately the Grand Duke himself escaped. In this fateful hour our carpet weavers, these eternal trouble-makers, had the audacity to incite a rebellion and hang our universally beloved city Judge, our dear Illa Orbeliani. Tut-tut. My friends, we need peace, peace, peace in Grusinia. And justice. Here I bring you my dear nephew, Bizergan Kazbeki. He's to be the new Judge, a talented fellow. I say: the people must decide.

THE FIRST IRONSHIRT: Does this mean we elect the Judge?

THE FAT PRINCE: Precisely. The people propose a talented fel-

low. Confer, my friends. *The Ironshirts confer.* Don't worry,
little fox. The job's yours. And once we've run the Grand
Duke to earth we won't have to kiss the rabble's arse any
more.

THE IRONSHIRTS *to each other*: They've got the jitters because
they still haven't caught the Grand Duke. – We've this
clerk to thank for that. He let him get away. – They're not
sure of things yet. So they say: 'My friends!' And: 'The
people must decide!' – Now he even wants justice for Grusinia! – But fun's fun as long as it lasts. – We'll ask the
clerk; he knows all about justice. Hey, scoundrel, would you
like to have the nephew as Judge?

AZDAK: You mean me?

THE FIRST IRONSHIRT *repeats*: Would you like to have the
nephew as Judge?

AZDAK: You asking me? You're not really asking me that, are
you?

THE SECOND IRONSHIRT: Why not? Anything for a laugh!

AZDAK: I take it you want him put to the test? Am I right?
Have you a crook on hand? An experienced one? So the
candidate can show how good he is?

THE THIRD IRONSHIRT: Let me see. We have the Governor's
tart's two doctors down there. Let's use them.

AZDAK: Stop! That's no good! You can't take real crooks till
we're sure of the Judge being appointed. He may be an ass,
but he must be appointed or else the law is violated. The
law is a very sensitive organ. Like the spleen. Once attacked
with fists, death occurs. You can hang those two. Why not?
You won't have violated the law, because no Judge was
present. Judgment must always be passed with complete
solemnity – because it's such rot. Suppose a Judge throws a
woman into clink for having stolen a corncake for her child.
And he isn't wearing his robes. Or he's scratching himself
while passing sentence so that more than a third of his body
is exposed – in which case he'd have to scratch his thigh –
then the sentence he passes is a disgrace and the law is
violated. It would be easier for a Judge's robe and a Judge's

hat to pass sentence than for a man without all that para-
phernalia. If you don't look out, the law goes up in smoke.
You don't taste wine by offering it to a dog. Why not?
Because the wine would be gone.

THE FIRST IRONSHIRT: So what do you suggest, you hair-splitter?

AZDAK: I'll be the defendant. I even know what sort. *Azdak
whispers to them.*

THE FIRST IRONSHIRT: You? *All burst out laughing.*

THE FAT PRINCE: What have you decided?

THE FIRST IRONSHIRT: We've decided to have a rehearsal. Our
good friend will act as defendant, and here's the Judge's seat
for the candidate.

THE FAT PRINCE: That's unusual. But why not? *To the nephew*:
A mere formality, little fox. What did they teach you? Who
gets there first? The slow runner or the fast one?

THE NEPHEW: The silent one, Uncle Arsen.

*The nephew sits in the Judge's seat, the fat prince standing behind
him. The Ironshirts sit on the steps. Enter Azdak, imitating the
unmistakable gait of the Grand Duke.*

AZDAK: Is there anyone here who knows me? I am the Grand
Duke.

THE FAT PRINCE: What is he?

THE SECOND IRONSHIRT: The Grand Duke. He really does
know him.

THE FAT PRINCE: Good.

THE FIRST IRONSHIRT: Get on with the proceedings.

AZDAK: Listen! I'm accused of war-mongering. Ridiculous! Am
saying: ridiculous! Is that enough? If not, have brought lawyers along. About 500. *He points behind him, pretending to be
surrounded by lawyers.* Requisition all available seats for lawyers. *The Ironshirts laugh; the fat prince joins in.*

THE NEPHEW *to the Ironshirts*: Do you want me to try this case?
I must admit I find it rather unusual. From the point of
view of taste, I mean.

THE FIRST IRONSHIRT: Go on.

THE FAT PRINCE *smiling*: Let him have it, little fox!

THE NEPHEW: All right. People of Grusinia versus Grand Duke. What have you to say, defendant?

AZDAK: Any amount. Of course, have myself read war lost. Started war at the time on advice of patriots like Uncle Kazbeki. Demand Uncle Kazbeki as witness. *The Ironshirts laugh.*

THE FAT PRINCE *to the Ironshirts, affably*: Queer fish, eh?

THE NEPHEW: Motion overruled. You're being accused not of declaring war, which every ruler has to do once in a while, but of conducting it badly.

AZDAK: Rot! Didn't conduct it at all! Had it conducted. Had it conducted by Princes! Made a mess of it, of course!

THE NEPHEW: Do you deny having been Commander in Chief?

AZDAK: Not at all! Always was Commander in Chief. Even at birth howled at wet-nurse; trained to drop turds in latrine. Got used to command. Always commanded officials to rob my cash-box. Officers flog soldiers only on my command. Landlords sleep with peasants' wives only when strictly commanded by me. Uncle Kazbeki here grew stomach only on my command.

THE IRONSHIRTS *clapping*: He's good! Up the Grand Duke!

THE FAT PRINCE: Answer him, little fox! I'm with you!

THE NEPHEW: I shall answer him according to the dignity of the law. Defendant, preserve the dignity of the law.

AZDAK: Agreed. Command you proceed with the trial.

THE NEPHEW: It's not your business to command me. So you claim the Princes forced you to declare war. Then how can you claim they made a mess of it?

AZDAK: Didn't send enough troops. Embezzled funds. Brought sick horses. During attack found drunk in whore-house. Propose Uncle Kaz as witness. *The Ironshirts laugh.*

THE NEPHEW: Are you making the outrageous claim that the Princes of this country did not fight?

AZDAK: No. Princes fought. Fought for war contracts.

THE FAT PRINCE *jumping up*: That's too much! This man talks like a carpet weaver!

AZDAK: Really? Only telling the truth!

71

THE FAT PRINCE: Hang him! Hang him!

THE FIRST IRONSHIRT: Keep quiet. Get on, Excellency.

THE NEPHEW: Quiet! Now pass sentence. Must be hanged. Hanged by the neck. Having lost war. Sentence passed. No appeal.

THE FAT PRINCE *hysterically*: Away with him! Away with him! Away with him!

AZDAK: Young man, seriously advise not to fall publicly into jerky, clipped manner of speech. Can't be employed as watch-dog if howl like wolf. Got it?

THE FAT PRINCE: Hang him!

AZDAK: If people realise Princes talk same language as Grand Dukes, may even hang Grand Dukes and Princes. By the way, sentence quashed. Reason: war lost, but not for Princes. Princes have won *their* war. Got themselves paid 3,863,000 piastres for horses not delivered.

THE FAT PRINCE: Hang him!

AZDAK: 8,240,000 piastres for food supplies not produced.

THE FAT PRINCE: Hang him!

AZDAK: Are therefore victors. War lost only for Grusinia, which is not present in this Court.

THE FAT PRINCE: I think that's enough, my friends. *To Azdak*: You can withdraw, gaol-bird. *To the Ironshirts*: I think you can now ratify the new Judge's appointment, my friends.

THE FIRST IRONSHIRT: Yes, we can do that. Take down the Judge's robe. *One of the Ironshirts climbs on the back of an-other and pulls the robe off the hanged man.* And now – *to the nephew* – you be off so that we can put the right arse on the right seat. *To Azdak*: Step forward, you, and sit on the Judge's seat. *Azdak hesitates.* Sit down up there, man. *Azdak is thrust on to the seat by the Ironshirts.* The Judge was always a rascal. Now the rascal shall be the Judge. *The Judge's robe is placed round his shoulders, the wicker from a bottle on his head.* Look! There's a Judge for you!

THE SINGER:

Now there was civil war in the land. The rulers were unsafe.

Now Azdak was made a Judge by the Ironshirts.
Now Azdak remained a Judge for two years.

THE SINGER WITH HIS MUSICIANS:
Great houses turn to ashes
And blood runs down the street.
Rats come out of the sewers
And maggots out of the meat.
The thug and the blasphemer
Lounge by the altar-stone:
Now, now, now Azdak
Sits on the Judgment throne.

Azdak sits on the Judge's seat peeling an apple. Shauva sweeps out the hall. On one side an invalid in a wheelchair, the accused doctor and a man in rags with a limp; opposite, a young man accused of blackmail. An Ironshirt stands on guard holding the Ironshirts' banner.

AZDAK: In view of the large number of cases, the Court today will hear two cases simultaneously. Before I open the proceedings, a short announcement: I receive – *he stretches out his hand; only the blackmailer produces some money and hands it to him* – I reserve for myself the right to punish one of these parties here – *he glances at the invalid* – for contempt of court. You – *to the doctor* – are a doctor, and you – *to the invalid* – are bringing a complaint against him. Is the doctor responsible for your condition?

THE INVALID: Yes. I had a stroke because of him.

AZDAK: That sounds like professional negligence.

THE INVALID: More than negligence. I gave this man money to study. So far he hasn't paid me back one penny. And when I heard he was treating a patient free, I had a stroke.

AZDAK: Rightly. *To the limping man.* And you, what do you want here?

THE LIMPING MAN: I'm the patient, your Worship.

AZDAK: He treated your leg?

THE LIMPING MAN: Not the right one. My rheumatism was in

73

the left leg, and he operated on my right. That's why I'm limping now.

AZDAK: And you got that free?

THE INVALID: A 500-piastre operation free! For nothing! For a God-Bless-You! And I paid this man's studies! *To the doctor*: Did you learn to operate for nothing at school?

THE DOCTOR *to Azdak*: Your Worship, it is actually the custom to demand the fee before the operation, as the patient is more willing to pay before an operation than after. Which is only human. In this case I was convinced, when I started the operation, that my servant had already received the fee. In this I was mistaken.

THE INVALID: He was mistaken! A good doctor doesn't make mistakes. He examines before he operates.

AZDAK: That's right. *To Shauva*: Public Prosecutor, what's the other case about?

SHAUVA *busily sweeping*: Blackmail.

THE BLACKMAILER: High Court of Justice, I'm innocent. I only wanted to find out from the landowner in question if he really had raped his niece. He kindly informed me that this was not the case, and gave me the money only so that I could let my uncle study music.

AZDAK: Ah ha! *To the doctor*: You on the other hand can't produce any extenuating circumstances in your defence?

THE DOCTOR: Except that to err is human.

AZDAK: And you know that in money matters a good doctor is conscious of his responsibility? I once heard of a doctor who made a thousand piastres out of one sprained finger: he discovered it had something to do with the circulation of the blood, which a less good doctor would have overlooked. On another occasion, by careful treatment, he turned a mediocre gall bladder into a gold mine. You have no excuse, Doctor. The corn merchant Uxu made his son study medicine to get some knowledge of trade – our medical schools are that good. *To the blackmailer*: What's the name of the landowner?

SHAUVA: He doesn't want it to be known.

AZDAK: In that case I will pass judgment. The Court considers

74

the blackmail proved. And you – *to the invalid* – are sentenced to a fine of 1000 piastres. If you get a second stroke the doctor will have to treat you free and if necessary amputate. *To the limping man*: As compensation, you will receive a bottle of embrocation! *To the blackmailer*: You are sentenced to hand over half the proceeds of your deal to the Public Prosecutor, to keep the landowner's name secret. You are advised, moreover, to study medicine. You seem well suited to that profession. And you, Doctor, are acquitted because of an inexcusable professional mistake. The next cases!

THE SINGER WITH HIS MUSICIANS:

> Beware of willing Judges
> For Truth is a black cat
> In a windowless room at midnight
> And Justice a blind bat.
> A third and shrugging party
> Alone can right our wrong.
> This, this, this, Azdak
> Does for a mere song.

Enter Azdak from the caravansary on the highway, followed by the old, bearded innkeeper. The Judge's seat is carried by manservants and Shauva. An Ironshirt with a banner takes up position.

AZDAK: Put it here. Then at least we can get some air and a little breeze from the lemon grove over there. It's good for Justice to do it in the open. The wind blows her skirts up and you can see what's underneath. Shauva, we have eaten too much. These rounds of inspection are very exhausting. *To the innkeeper*: So it's about your daughter-in-law?

THE INNKEEPER: Your Worship, it's about the family honour. I wish to bring an action on behalf of my son, who's gone on business across the mountain. This is the offending stableman, and here's my unfortunate daughter-in-law.

Enter the daughter-in-law, a voluptuous wench. She is veiled.

AZDAK *sitting down*: I receive. *Sighing, the innkeeper hands him some money*. Good. Now the formalities are disposed of. This is a case of rape?

75

THE INNKEEPER: Your Worship, I surprised this rascal in the stable in the act of laying our Ludovica in the straw.

AZDAK: Quite right, the stable. Beautiful horses. I particularly like the little roan.

THE INNKEEPER: The first thing I did of course was to berate Ludovica on behalf of my son.

AZDAK *seriously*: I said I liked the little roan.

THE INNKEEPER *coldly*: Really? – Ludovica admitted that the stableman took her against her will.

AZDAK: Take off your veil, Ludovica. *She does so.* Ludovica, you please the Court. Tell us how it happened.

LUDOVICA *as though well rehearsed*: When I entered the stable to look at the new foal, the stableman said to me of his own accord: 'It's hot today' and laid his hand on my left breast. I said to him: 'Don't do that!' But he continued to handle me indecently, which provoked my anger. Before I realised his sinful intentions, he became intimate with me. It had already happened when my father-in-law entered and accidentally trod on me.

THE INNKEEPER *explaining*: On behalf of my son.

AZDAK *to the stableman*: Do you admit that you started it?

THE STABLEMAN: Yes.

AZDAK: Ludovica, do you like to eat sweet things?

LUDOVICA: Yes, sunflower seeds.

AZDAK: Do you like sitting a long time in the tub?

LUDOVICA: Half an hour or so.

AZDAK: Public Prosecutor, just drop your knife on the floor. *Shauva does so.* Ludovica, go and pick up the Public Prosecutor's knife.

Ludovica, hips swaying, goes and picks up the knife.

Azdak points at her. Do you see that? The way it sways? The criminal element has been discovered. The rape has been proved. By eating too much, especially sweet things, by lying too long in warm water, by laziness and too soft a skin, you have raped the poor man. Do you imagine you can go around with a bottom like that and get away with it in Court? This

is a case of deliberate assault with a dangerous weapon. You
are sentenced to hand over to the Court the little roan which
your father liked to ride on behalf of his son. And now,
Ludovica, come with me to the stable so that the Court may
investigate the scene of the crime.

Azdak is carried on his Judge's seat by Ironshirts from place to place
on the Grusinian highway. Behind him come Shauva dragging the
gallows and the stableman leading the little roan.

THE SINGER WITH HIS MUSICIANS:
  No more did the Lower Orders
   Tremble in their shoes
  At the bellows of their Betters
   At *Come-Here*'s and *Listen-You*'s.
  His balances were crooked
   But they shouted in the streets: -
  'Good, good, good is Azdak
   And the measure that he metes!'

  He took them from Wealthy Peter
   To give to Penniless Paul
  Sealed his illegal judgments
   With a waxen tear, and all
  The rag-tag-and-bobtail
   Ran crying up and down: -
  'Cheer, cheer, cheer for Azdak
   The darling of the town!'

The little group slowly withdraws.

  To love your next-door neighbour
   Approach him with an axe
  For prayers and saws and sermons
   Are unconvincing facts.
  What miracles of preaching
   A good sharp blade can do:
  So, so, so, so Azdak
   Makes miracles come true.

Azdak's Judge's seat is in a tavern. Three farmers stand before
Azdak. Shauva brings him wine. In a corner stands an old peasant

CCC F   77

woman. In the open doorway, and outside, stand villagers and spectators. An Ironshirt stands guard with a banner.

AZDAK: The Public Prosecutor opens the proceedings.

SHAUVA: It's about a cow. For five weeks the defendant has had a cow in her stable, the property of farmer Suru. She was also found to be in the possession of a stolen ham. And cows belonging to farmer Shutoff were killed after he had asked the defendant to pay the rent for a field.

THE FARMERS: It's about my ham, Your Worship. – It's about my cow, Your Worship. – It's about my field, Your Worship.

AZDAK: Granny, what have you got to say to all this?

THE OLD WOMAN: Your Worship, one night towards morning, five weeks ago, there was a knock at my door, and outside stood a bearded man with a cow. He said, 'Dear woman, I am the miracle-working St Banditus. And because your son has been killed in the war, I bring you this cow as a keepsake. Take good care of it!'

THE FARMERS: The robber Irakli, Your Worship! – Her brother-in-law, Your Worship! The cattle thief, the incendiary! – He must be beheaded!

Outside a woman screams. The crowd grows restless and retreats. Enter the bandit Irakli, with a huge axe.

THE FARMERS: Irakli! *They cross themselves.*

THE BANDIT: A very good evening, dear friends! A glass of wine!

AZDAK: Public Prosecutor, a jug of wine for the guest. And who are you?

THE BANDIT: I'm a wandering hermit, Your Worship. And thank you for the kind gift. *He empties the glass which Shauva has brought.* Same again!

AZDAK: I'm Azdak. *He gets up and bows. The bandit also bows.* The Court welcomes the stranger hermit. Go on with your story, Granny.

THE OLD WOMAN: Your Worship, that first night I didn't know that St Banditus could work miracles, it was only the cow. But one night a few days later the farmer's servants came to take the cow away from me. Then they turned round in front of my door and went off without the cow. And on their heads sprouted bumps big as a fist. Then I knew that St Banditus had changed their hearts and turned them into friendly people.

The bandit roars with laughter.

THE FIRST FARMER: I know what changed them.

AZDAK: That's good. You can tell us later. Continue.

THE OLD WOMAN: Your Worship, the next one to become a good man was farmer Shutoff – a devil, as everyone knows. But St Banditus brought it about that Shutoff let me off paying the rent for the field.

THE SECOND FARMER: Because my cows were killed in the field.

The bandit laughs.

THE OLD WOMAN *answering Azdak's sign to continue*: And then one morning the ham came flying in at my window. It hit me in the small of the back. I've been lame ever since. Look, Your Worship. *She limps a few steps. The bandit laughs.* I ask Your Worship: when was a poor old body ever given a ham except by a miracle?

The bandit starts sobbing.

AZDAK *rising from his seat*: Granny, that's a question that strikes straight at the Court's heart. Be so kind as to sit down here.

Hesitating, the old woman sits on the Judge's seat. Azdak sits on the floor, glass in hand.

> Little mother, I almost called you Mother Grusinia, the woebegone
> The bereaved one, whose sons are in the war.
> Who is beaten with fists, but full of hope.
> Who weeps when she is given a cow
> And is surprised when she is not beaten.
> Little mother, pass merciful sentence on us, the damned!

He bellows to the farmers.

> Admit that you don't believe in miracles, you atheists! Each of you is sentenced to pay 500 piastres! For your lack of faith. Get out!

The farmers creep out.

And you, little mother, and you – *to the bandit* – pious man, drink a jug of wine with the Public Prosecutor and Azdak!

THE SINGER WITH HIS MUSICIANS:
> To feed the starving people
>> He broke the laws like bread
>
> There on the seat of justice
>> With the gallows over his head
>
> For more than seven hundred
>> Days he calmed their wails
>
> Well, well, well, did Azdak
>> Measure with false scales.

> Two summers and two winters
>> A poor man judged the poor
>
> And on the wreck of justice
>> He brought them safe to shore
>
> For he spoke in the mob language
>> That the mob understands.
>
> I, I, I, cried Azdak
>> Take bribes from empty hands.

THE SINGER:
> Then the era of disorder was over, the Grand Duke returned
>
> The Governor's wife returned, a Judgment was held.
>
> Many people died, the suburbs burned anew, and fear seized Azdak.

Azdak's Judge's seat stands again in the Court of Justice. Azdak sits on the ground mending a shoe and talking to Shauva. Noises outside. Above a wall the fat prince's head is carried by on a lance.

AZDAK: Shauva, your days of slavery are numbered, perhaps even the minutes. For a long time I have held you on the iron curb of reason, and it has made your mouth bloody. I have lashed you with arguments founded on reason, and ill-treated you with logic. You are by nature a weak creature, and if one slyly throws you an argument, you have to devour it; you can't resist. By nature you are compelled to lick the hand of a superior being, but superior beings can be very different. And now comes your liberation, and you will soon be able to follow your inclinations, which are low. You will be able to follow your unerring instinct, which teaches you to plant your heavy boot on the faces of men. Gone is the era of confusion and disorder, and the great times which I found described in the Song of Chaos have not yet come. Let us now sing that song together in memory of those wonderful days. Sit down and don't violate the music. Don't be afraid. It sounds all right. It has a popular refrain.

He sings:

> Sister, hide your face; brother, take your knife, the times are out of joint.
> The noblemen are full of complaints, the simple folk full of joy.
> The city says: let us drive the strong ones out of our midst
> Storm the government buildings, destroy the lists of the serfs.
> Now the masters' noses are put to the grindstone. Those who never saw the day have emerged.
> The poor-boxes of ebony are broken, the precious sesame wood is used for beds.
> He who lacked bread now possesses barns; he who lived on the corn of charity, now measures it out himself.

SHAUVA: Oh, oh, oh, oh.

AZDAK:

> Where are you, General? Please, please, please, restore order.
> The son of the nobleman can no longer be recognised; the child of the mistress becomes the son of her slave.
> The councillors are taking shelter in the barn; he who was barely allowed to sleep on the wall now lolls in bed.
> He who once rowed a boat now owns ships; when their owner looks for them, they are no longer his.
> Five men are sent out by their master. They say: go yourself, we have arrived.

SHAUVA: Oh, oh, oh, oh.

AZDAK:

> Where are you, General? Please, please, please restore
> order!

Yes, so it might have been, if order had been much longer
neglected. But now the Grand Duke, whose life I saved like
a fool, has returned to the Capital. And the Persians have lent
him an army to restore order. The outer town is already in
flames. Go and get me the Big Book I like to sit on. *Shauva
brings the book from the Judge's seat. Azdak opens it.* This is
the Statute Book and I've always used it, as you can confirm.

SHAUVA: Yes, to sit on.

AZDAK: Now I'd better look and see what they can do to me,
because I've always allowed the have-nots to get away with
everything. And I'll have to pay for it dearly. I helped to put
Poverty on to its rickety legs, so they'll hang me for drunken-
ness. I peeped into the rich man's pocket, which is considered
bad taste. And I can't hide anywhere, for all the world knows
me, since I have helped the world.

SHAUVA: Someone's coming!

AZDAK *in a panic walks trembling to the seat*: The game is up!
But I'll give no man the pleasure of seeing human greatness.
I'll beg on my knees for mercy. Spittle will slobber down my
chin. The fear of death is upon me.

*Enter Natella Abashvili, the Governor's wife, followed by the Ad-
jutant and an Ironshirt.*

THE GOVERNOR'S WIFE: What kind of a man is that, Shalva?

AZDAK: A willing one, Your Excellency, a man ready to oblige.

THE ADJUTANT: Natella Abashvili, wife of the late Governor,
has just returned and is looking for her three-year-old son,
Michael. She has been informed that the child was abducted
to the mountains by a former servant.

AZDAK: It will be brought back, Your Highness, at your service.

THE ADJUTANT: They say that the person in question is passing
it off as her own child.

AZDAK: She will be beheaded, Your Highness, at your service.

THE ADJUTANT: That's all.

THE GOVERNOR'S WIFE *leaving*: I don't like that man.

AZDAK *following her to the door, and bowing*: Everything will be
arranged, Your Highness, at your service.

6

THE CHALK CIRCLE

THE SINGER:

> Now listen to the story of the trial concerning the child of
> the Governor Abashvili
> To establish the true mother
> By the famous test of the Chalk Circle.

*The Court of Justice in Nukha. Ironshirts lead Michael in, then
go across the stage and out at the back. One Ironshirt holds Grusha
back under the doorway with his lance until the child has been taken
away. Then she is admitted. She is accompanied by the former
Governor's cook. Distant noises and a fire-red sky.*

GRUSHA: He's so good, he can wash himself already.

THE COOK: You're lucky. This is not a real Judge; this is Azdak.
He's a drunk and doesn't understand anything. And the big-
gest thieves have been acquitted by him, because he mixes
everything up and because the rich never offer him big enough
bribes. The likes of us get off lightly sometimes.

GRUSHA: I need some luck today.

THE COOK: Touch wood. *She crosses herself.* I think I'd better
say a quick prayer that the Judge will be drunk.

*Her lips move in prayer, while Grusha looks round in vain for the
child.*

THE COOK: What I can't understand is why you want to hold on
to it at any price, if it's not yours. In these days.

GRUSHA: It's mine, I've brought it up.

THE COOK: But have you never wondered what'll happen when
she returns?

GRUSHA: At first I thought I'd give it back to her. Then I thought she wouldn't return.

THE COOK: And a borrowed coat keeps one warm, too, eh? *Grusha nods.* I'll swear anything you like, because you're a decent person. *Memorises aloud*: I had him in my care for five piastres, and on Thursday evening, when the riots started, Grusha came to fetch him. *She sees the soldier, Chachava, approaching*. But you have done Simon great wrong. I've talked to him. He can't understand it.

GRUSHA *unaware of Simon's presence*: I can't be bothered with that man just now, if he doesn't understand anything.

THE COOK: He has understood that the child is not yours, but that you're married and won't be free until death parts you – he can't understand that.

Grusha sees Simon and greets him.

SIMON *gloomily*: I wanted to tell the woman that I am ready to swear I am the father of the child.

GRUSHA *low*: That's right, Simon.

SIMON: At the same time, I would like to say that I am hereby not bound to anything; nor the woman, either.

THE COOK: That's unnecessary. She's married. You know that.

SIMON: That's her business and doesn't need rubbing in.

Enter two Ironshirts.

THE IRONSHIRTS: Where's the Judge? – Has anyone seen the Judge?

GRUSHA *who has turned away and covered her face*: Stand in front of me. I shouldn't have come to Nukha. If I run into the Ironshirt, the one I hit over the head . . .

The Ironshirt who has brought in the child steps forward.

THE IRONSHIRT: The Judge isn't here.

The two Ironshirts go on searching.

THE COOK: I hope something hasn't happened to him. With any other Judge you'd have less chance than a chicken has teeth.

Enter another Ironshirt.

84

THE IRONSHIRT *who had enquired for the Judge, to the other Iron-shirt*: There are only two old people and a child here. The Judge has bolted.

THE OTHER IRONSHIRT: Go on searching!

The first two Ironshirts go out quickly. The third remains behind. Grusha lets out a scream. The Ironshirt turns round. He is the Corporal, and has a large scar right across his face.

THE IRONSHIRT *in the gateway*: What's the matter, Shotta? Do you know her?

THE CORPORAL *after a long stare*: No.

THE IRONSHIRT: She's the one who's supposed to have stolen the Abashvili child. If you know anything about it, Shotta, you can make a packet of money.

Exit the Corporal, cursing.

THE COOK: Was it him? *Grusha nods.* I think he'll keep his mouth shut, otherwise he'll have to admit he was after the child.

GRUSHA *relieved*: I'd almost forgotten I'd saved the child from them . . .

Enter the Governor's wife, followed by the Adjutant and two lawyers.

THE GOVERNOR'S WIFE: Thank God! At least the common people aren't here. I can't stand their smell, it always gives me migraine.

THE FIRST LAWYER: Madam, I must ask you to be as careful as possible in everything you say, until we have another Judge.

THE GOVERNOR'S WIFE: But I didn't say anything, Illo Shubo-ladze. I love the people – with their simple, straightforward ways. It's just their smell that brings on my migraine.

THE SECOND LAWYER: There will hardly be any spectators. Most of the population is behind locked doors because of the riots in the outer town.

THE GOVERNOR'S WIFE *looking at Grusha*: Is that the creature?

THE FIRST LAWYER: I beg you, most gracious Natella Abashvili, to abstain from all invective until it is absolutely certain that the Grand Duke has appointed a new Judge and we have got rid of the present one, who is about the lowest ever seen in a Judge's robe. And things seem to be on the move, as you will see.

Ironshirts enter the courtyard.

THE COOK: Her Ladyship wouldn't hesitate to pull your hair out if she didn't know that Azdak is for the poor people. He goes by the face.

Two Ironshirts begin by fastening a rope to the pillar. Azdak, in chains, is led in, followed by Shauva, also in chains. The three farmers bring up the rear.

ONE IRONSHIRT: Trying to run away, eh? *He beats Azdak.*
ONE FARMER: Pull the Judge's robe off before we string him up!

Ironshirts and farmers pull the robe off Azdak. His torn underwear becomes visible. Then someone kicks him.

AN IRONSHIRT *pushing him on to someone else*: Anyone want a bundle of Justice? Here it is!

Accompanied by shouts of 'It's all yours!' and 'I don't want it!' they hurl Azdak back and forth until he breaks down. Then he is hauled up and dragged under the noose.

THE GOVERNOR'S WIFE *who, during the 'ball-game', has been clapping her hands hysterically*: I disliked that man from the moment I first saw him.
AZDAK *covered in blood, panting*: I can't see. Give me a rag.
THE OTHER IRONSHIRT: What is it you want to see?
AZDAK: You, you dogs! *He wipes the blood out of his eyes with his shirt.* Good morning, dogs! How are you, dogs? How's the dog world? Does it stink good? Have you got another boot to lick? Are you back at each other's throats, dogs?

Enter a dust-covered rider accompanied by a corporal. He takes some documents from a leather case and looks through them. He interrupts.

THE RIDER: Stop! I bring a despatch from the Grand Duke, containing the latest appointments.

THE CORPORAL *bellows*: Atten – shun!

All jump to attention.

THE RIDER: Of the new Judge it says: We appoint a man whom we have to thank for the saving of a life of the utmost importance to the country. A certain Azdak in Nukha. Which is he?

SHAUVA *pointing*: That's him on the gallows, Your Excellency.

THE CORPORAL *bellowing*: What's going on here?

THE IRONSHIRT: I ask to be allowed to report that His Worship has already been His Worship. He was declared the enemy of the Grand Duke only on these farmers' denunciation.

THE CORPORAL *pointing at the farmers*: March them off! *They are marched off, bowing incessantly.* See to it that His Worship is exposed to no more indignities.

Exit the rider with the corporal.

THE COOK *to Shauva*: She clapped her hands! I hope he saw it!

THE FIRST LAWYER: This is a catastrophe.

Azdak has fainted. Coming to, he is dressed again in a Judge's robe. He walks away, swaying, from the group of Ironshirts.

THE IRONSHIRTS: Don't take it amiss, Your Worship. What are Your Worship's wishes?

AZDAK: Nothing, fellow dogs. An occasional boot to lick. *To Shauva*: I pardon you. *He is unchained.* Fetch me some of the red wine. The sweetest. *Exit Shauva.* Get out of here, I've got to judge a case. *The Ironshirts go. Shauva returns with a jug of wine. Azdak takes deep gulps.* Get me something for my backside. *Shauva brings the Statute Book and puts it on the Judge's seat. Azdak sits on it.* I receive! *The faces of the prosecutors, among whom a worried council has been held, show smiles of relief. They whisper.*

THE COOK: Oh dear!

SIMON: 'A well can't be filled with dew!' they say.

THE LAWYERS *approaching Azdak, who stands up expectantly*: An absolutely ridiculous case, Your Worship. The accused has abducted the child and refuses to hand it over.

AZDAK *stretching out his hand, and glancing at Grusha*: A most

87

attractive person. *He receives more money.* I open the proceedings and demand the absolute truth. *To Grusha*: Especially from you.

THE FIRST LAWYER: High Court of Justice! Blood, as the saying goes, is thicker than water. This old proverb . . .

AZDAK: The Court wants to know the lawyer's fee.

THE FIRST LAWYER *surprised*: I beg your pardon? *Azdak rubs his thumb and index finger.* Oh, I see. 500 piastres, Your Worship, is the answer to the Court's somewhat unusual question.

AZDAK: Did you hear? The question is unusual. I ask it because I listen to you in a quite different way if I know you are good.

THE FIRST LAWYER *bowing*: Thank you, Your Worship. Hgh Court of Justice! Of all bonds the bonds of blood are the strongest. Mother and child – is there a more intimate relationship? Can one tear a child from its mother? High Court of Justice! She has conceived it in the holy ecstasies of love. She has carried it in her womb. She has fed it with her blood. She has borne it with pain. High Court of Justice! It has been observed, Your Worship, how even the wild tigress, robbed of her young, roams restless through the mountains, reduced to a shadow. Nature herself . . .

AZDAK *interrupting, to Grusha*: What's your answer to all this and anything else the lawyer might have to say?

GRUSHA: He's mine.

AZDAK: Is that all? I hope you can prove it. In any case, I advise you to tell me why you think the child should be given to you.

GRUSHA: I've brought him up 'according to my best knowledge and conscience'. I always found him something to eat. Most of the time he had a roof over his head. And I went to all sorts of trouble for him. I had expenses, too. I didn't think of my own comfort. I brought up the child to be friendly with everyone. And from the beginning I taught him to work as well as he could. But he's still very small.

THE FIRST LAWYER: Your Worship, it is significant that the person herself doesn't claim any bond of blood between herself and this child.

AZDAK: The Court takes note.

THE FIRST LAWYER: Thank you, Your Worship. Please permit a woman who has suffered much – who has already lost her husband and now also has to fear the loss of her child – to address a few words to you. Her Highness, Natella Abashvili . . .

THE GOVERNOR'S WIFE *quietly*: A most cruel fate, sir, forces me to ask you to return my beloved child. It's not for me to describe to you the tortures of a bereaved mother's soul, the anxiety, the sleepless nights, the . . .

THE SECOND LAWYER *exploding*: It's outrageous the way this woman is treated. She's not allowed to enter her husband's palace. The revenue of her estates is blocked. She is told cold-bloodedly that it's tied to the heir. She can't do anything without the child. She can't even pay her lawyers. *To the first lawyer who, desperate about this outburst, makes frantic gestures to stop him speaking*: Dear Illo Shuboladze, why shouldn't it be divulged now that it's the Abashvili estates that are at stake?

THE FIRST LAWYER: Please, Honoured Sandro Obolodze! We had agreed . . . *To Azdak*: Of course it is correct that the trial will also decide whether our noble client will obtain the right to dispose of the large Abashvili estates. I say 'also' on purpose, because in the foreground stands the human tragedy of a mother, as Natella Abashvili has rightly explained at the beginning of her moving statement. Even if Michael Abashvili were *not* the heir to the estates, he would still be the dearly beloved child of my client.

AZDAK: Stop! The Court is touched by the mention of the estates. It's a proof of human feeling.

THE SECOND LAWYER: Thanks, Your Worship. Dear Illo Shuboladze, in any case we can prove that the person who took possession of the child is not the child's mother. Permit me to lay before the Court the bare facts. By an unfortunate chain of circumstances, the child, Michael Abashvili, was left behind while his mother was making her escape. Grusha, the Palace kitchenmaid, was present on this Easter Sunday and was observed busying herself with the child . . .

THE COOK: All her mistress was thinking about was what kind of dresses she would take along.

THE SECOND LAWYER *unmoved*: Almost a year later Grusha turned up in a mountain village with a child, and there entered into matrimony with . . .

AZDAK: How did you get into that mountain village?

GRUSHA: On foot, Your Worship. And he was mine.

SIMON: I am the father, Your Worship.

THE COOK: I had him in my care for five piastres, Your Worship.

THE SECOND LAWYER: This man is engaged to Grusha, High Court of Justice, and for this reason his testimony is not reliable.

AZDAK: Are you the man she married in the mountain village?

SIMON: No, Your Worship, she married a peasant.

AZDAK *winking at Grusha*: Why? *Pointing at Simon*: Isn't he any good in bed? Tell the truth.

GRUSHA: We didn't get that far. I married because of the child, so that he should have a roof over his head. *Pointing at Simon*. He was in the war, Your Worship.

AZDAK: And now he wants you again, eh?

SIMON: I want to state in evidence . . .

GRUSHA *angrily*: I am no longer free, Your Worship.

AZDAK: And the child, you claim, is the result of whoring? *Grusha does not answer*. I'm going to ask you a question: What kind of child is it? Is it one of those ragged street-urchins? Or is it a child from a well-to-do family?

GRUSHA *angrily*: It's an ordinary child.

AZDAK: I mean, did he have fine features from the beginning?

GRUSHA: He had a nose in his face.

AZDAK: He had a nose in his face. I consider that answer of yours to be important. They say of me that once, before passing judgment, I went out and sniffed at a rosebush. Tricks of this kind are necessary nowadays. I'll cut things short now, and listen no longer to your lies. *To Grusha*: Especially yours. *To the group of defendants*: I can imagine what you've cooked up between you to cheat me. I know you. You're swindlers.

GRUSHA *suddenly*: I can quite understand your wanting to cut it short, having seen what you received!

AZDAK: Shut up! Did I receive anything from you?

GRUSHA *while the cook tries to restrain her*: Because I haven't got anything.

AZDAK: Quite true. I never get a thing from starvelings. I might just as well starve myself. You want justice, but do you want to pay for it? When you go to the butcher you know you have to pay. But to the Judge you go as though to a funeral supper.

SIMON *loudly*: 'When the horse was shod, the horsefly stretched out its leg', as the saying is.

AZDAK *eagerly accepting the challenge*: 'Better a treasure in the sewer than a stone in the mountain stream.'

SIMON: ' "A fine day. Let's go fishing," said the angler to the worm.'

AZDAK: ' "I'm my own master," said the servant, and cut off his foot.'

SIMON: '"I love you like a father," said the Czar to the peasant, and had the Czarevitch's head chopped off.'

AZDAK: 'The fool's worst enemy is himself.'

SIMON: But 'a fart has no nose'.

AZDAK: Fined ten piastres for indecent language in Court. That'll teach you what Justice is.

GRUSHA: That's a fine kind of Justice. You jump on us because we don't talk so refined as that lot with their lawyers.

AZDAK: Exactly. The likes of you are too stupid. It's only right that you should get it in the neck.

GRUSHA: Because you want to pass the child on to her. She who is too refined even to know how to change its nappies! You don't know any more about Justice than I do, that's clear.

AZDAK: There's something in that. I'm an ignorant man. I haven't even a decent pair of trousers under my robe. See for yourself. With me, everything goes on food and drink. I was educated in a convent school. Come to think of it, I'll fine you ten piastres, too. For contempt of Court. What's more, you're a very silly girl to turn me against you, instead of making eyes at me and wagging your backside a bit to keep me in a good temper. Twenty piastres!

GRUSHA: Even if it were thirty, I'd tell you what I think of your justice, you drunken onion! How dare you talk to me as though you were the cracked Isaiah on the church window! When they pulled you out of your mother, it wasn't planned that you'd rap her over the knuckles for pinching a little bowl of corn from somewhere! Aren't you ashamed of yourself when you see how afraid I am of you? But you've let yourself become their servant. So that their houses are not taken away, because they've stolen them. Since when do houses belong to bed-bugs? But you're on the look-out, otherwise they couldn't drag our men into their wars. You bribe-taker!

Azdak gets up. He begins to beam. With a little hammer he knocks on the table half-heartedly as if to get silence. But as Grusha's scolding continues, he only beats time with it.

I've no respect for you. No more than for a thief or a murderer with a knife, who does what he wants. You can take the child away from me, a hundred against one, but I tell you one thing: for a profession like yours, they ought to choose only bloodsuckers and men who rape children. As a punishment. To make them sit in judgment over their fellow men, which is worse than swinging from the gallows.

AZDAK *sitting down*: Now it will be thirty! And I won't go on brawling with you as though we were in a tavern. What would happen to my dignity as a Judge? I've lost all interest in your case. Where's the couple who wanted a divorce? *To Shauva*: Bring them in. This case is adjourned for fifteen minutes.

THE FIRST LAWYER *to the Governor's wife*: Without producing any more evidence, Madam, we have the verdict in the bag.

THE COOK *to Grusha*: You've gone and spoiled your chances with him. You won't get the child now.

Enter a very old couple.

THE GOVERNOR'S WIFE: Shalva, my smelling salts!

AZDAK: I receive. *The old couple do not understand.* I hear you want to be divorced. How long have you been living together?

THE OLD WOMAN: Forty years, Your Worship.

AZDAK: And why d'you want a divorce?

THE OLD MAN: We don't like each other, Your Worship.

AZDAK: Since when?

THE OLD WOMAN: Oh, from the very beginning, Your Worship.

AZDAK: I'll consider your case and deliver my verdict when I'm finished with the other one. *Shauva leads them into the background.* I need the child. *He beckons Grusha towards him and bends not unkindly towards her.* I've noticed that you have a soft spot for justice. I don't believe he's your child, but if he were yours, woman, wouldn't you want him to be rich? You'd only have to say he isn't yours and at once he'd have a palace, scores of horses in his stable, scores of beggars on his doorstep, scores of soldiers in his service, and scores of petitioners in his courtyard. Now, what d'you say? Don't you want him to be rich?

Grusha is silent.

THE SINGER: Listen now to what the angry girl thought, but didn't say:

He sings:

> He who wears the shoes of gold
> Tramples on the weak and old
> Does evil all day long
> And mocks at wrong.

> O to carry as one's own
> Heavy is the heart of stone.
> The power to do ill
> Wears out the will.

> Hunger he will dread
> Not those who go unfed:
> Fear the fall of night
> But not the light.

AZDAK: I think I understand you, woman.

GRUSHA: I won't give him away. I've brought him up, and he knows me.

Enter Shauva with the child.

THE GOVERNOR'S WIFE: It's in rags!

GRUSHA: That's not true. I wasn't given the time to put on his good shirt.

THE GOVERNOR'S WIFE: It's been in a pig-stye.

GRUSHA *furious*: I'm no pig, but there are others who are. Where did you leave your child?

THE GOVERNOR'S WIFE: I'll let you have it, you vulgar person. *She is about to throw herself on Grusha, but is restrained by her lawyers.* She's a criminal! She must be whipped!

THE SECOND LAWYER *holding his hand over her mouth*: Most gracious Natella Abashvili, you promised . . . Your Worship, the plaintiff's nerves . . .

AZDAK: Plaintiff and defendant! The Court has listened to your case, and has come to no decision as to who the real mother of this child is. I as Judge have the duty of choosing a mother for the child. I'll make a test. Shauva, get a piece of chalk and draw a circle on the floor. *Shauva does so.* Now place the child in the centre. *Shauva puts Michael, who smiles at Grusha, in the centre of the circle.* Stand near the circle, both of you. *The Governor's wife and Grusha step up to the circle.* Now each of you take the child by a hand. The true mother is she who has the strength to pull the child out of the circle, towards herself.

THE SECOND LAWYER *quickly*: High Court of Justice, I protest! I object that the fate of the great Abashvili estates, which are bound up with the child as the heir, should be made dependent on such a doubtful wrestling match. Moreover, my client does not command the same physical strength as this person, who is accustomed to physical work.

AZDAK: She looks pretty well fed to me. Pull!

The Governor's wife pulls the child out of the circle to her side Grusha has let it go and stands aghast.

THE FIRST LAWYER *congratulating the Governor's wife*: What did I say! The bonds of blood!

AZDAK *to Grusha*: What's the matter with you? You didn't pull!

GRUSHA: I didn't hold on to him. *She runs to Azdak.* Your Worship, I take back everything I said against you. I ask your forgiveness. If I could just keep him until he can speak properly. He knows only a few words.

AZDAK: Don't influence the Court! I bet you know only twenty yourself. All right, I'll do the test once more, to make certain.

The two women take up positions again.

AZDAK: Pull!

Again Grusha lets go of the child.

GRUSHA *in despair*: I've brought him up! Am I to tear him to pieces? I can't do it!

AZDAK *rising*: And in this manner the Court has established the true mother. *To Grusha*: Take your child and be off with it. I advise you not to stay in town with him. *To the Governor's wife*: And you disappear before I fine you for fraud. Your estates fall to the city. A playground for children will be made out of them. They need one, and I have decided it shall be called after me – The Garden of Azdak.

The Governor's wife has fainted and is carried out by the Adjutant. Her lawyers have preceded her. Grusha stands motionless. Shauva leads the child towards her.

AZDAK: Now I'll take off this Judge's robe – it has become too hot for me. I'm not cut out for a hero. But I invite you all to a little farewell dance, outside on the meadow. Oh, I had almost forgotten something in my excitement. I haven't signed the decree for divorce.

Using the Judge's seat as a table, he writes something on a piece of paper and prepares to leave. Dance music has started.

SHAUVA *having read what is on the paper*: But that's not right. You haven't divorced the old couple. You've divorced Grusha from her husband.

95

AZDAK: Have I divorced the wrong ones? I'm sorry, but it'll have to stand. I never retract anything. If I did, there'd be no law and order. *To the old couple*: Instead, I'll invite you to my feast. You won't mind dancing with each other. *To Grusha and Simon*: I've still got 40 piastres coming from you.

SIMON *pulling out his purse*: That's cheap, Your Worship. And many thanks.

AZDAK *pocketing the money*: I'll need it.

GRUSHA: So we'd better leave town tonight, eh, Michael? *About to take the child on her back. To Simon*: You like him?

SIMON *taking the child on his back*: With my respects, I like him.

GRUSHA: And now I can tell you: I took him because on that Easter Sunday I got engaged to you. And so it is a child of love. Michael, let's dance.

She dances with Michael. Simon dances with the cook. The old couple dance with each other. Azdak stands lost in thought. The dancers soon hide him from view. Occasionally he is seen again, but less and less as more couples enter and join the dance.

THE SINGER:

> And after this evening Azdak disappeared and was never seen again.
> But the people of Grusinia did not forget him and often remembered
> His time of Judgment as a brief
> Golden Age that was almost just.

The dancing couples dance out. Azdak has disappeared.

> But you, who have listened to the story of the Chalk Circle
> Take note of the meaning of the ancient song:
> That what there is shall belong to those who are good for it, thus
> The children to the maternal, that they thrive;
> The carriages to good drivers, that they are driven well;
> And the valley to the waterers, that it shall bear fruit.

Music.